GLOBAL RESET

GLOBAL RESET

DO CURRENT EVENTS POINT TO THE ANTICHRIST AND HIS WORLDWIDE EMPIRE?

MARK HITCHCOCK AND JEFF KINLEY

W PUBLISHING GROUP

AN IMPRINT OF THOMAS NELSON

Published in Nashville, Tennessee, by W Publishing, an imprint of Thomas Nelson.

Thomas Nelson titles may be purchased in bulk for educational, business, fundraising, or sales promotional use. For information, please email SpecialMarkets@ThomasNelson.com.

ISBN 978-0-7852-8976-0 (audiobook)
ISBN 978-0-7852-8953-1 (eBook)
ISBN 978-0-7852-8943-2 (TP)

Library of Congress Cataloging-in-Publication Data

Library of Congress Control Number: 2021947719

Printed in the United States of America

22 23 24 25 26 LSC 10 9 8 7 6 5 4 3

CONTENTS

ONE

GLOBAL *PRE*-SET

On Sunday night, March 18, 1990, in Boston, Massachusetts, two security guards faithfully stood at their posts keeping an uneventful watch over the famed Isabella Stewart Gardner Museum. Inside the building, a lifetime collection of masterpieces was carefully housed and protected. But all of that was about to change.

At 1:20 a.m. there was an unexpected knock on the museum's side door. Security guard Richard "Rick" Abath answered the door to discover two Boston police officers standing there. The officers explained that they were there to investigate a noise complaint. Without hesitation, Abath dutifully buzzed the officers in, whereupon they announced to the two security guards, "Gentlemen, this is a robbery."

Within eleven minutes, Abath and his coworker found themselves handcuffed, blindfolded, and locked away in the museum's basement.

Now with free rein in the building, the two armed robbers

proceeded to snatch paintings, breaking their protective glass cases and cutting them out of the frames. In eighty-one minutes, the duo had rounded up an assortment of artwork, including Rembrandt's *The Storm on the Sea of Galilee*, *A Lady and Gentleman in Black*, and *Self-Portrait*. Also taken were Johannes Vermeer's *The Concert*, sketches by Edgar Degas, and a famous work by Édouard Manet.

The next morning, the two museum guards were discovered still bound in the basement, and the damage assessment began.

During the ensuing investigation, it was determined that the thieves almost certainly had no real expertise in art, as some of the museum's most priceless items were left untouched. Even so, after all was said and done, the two robbers managed to steal half a billion dollars' worth of the world's finest paintings and drawings. It is a story worthy of a true crime mystery novel or a Hollywood movie. Sadly, the stolen artwork has never been found, despite a $10 million reward for information leading to its safe recovery.

To date, the Isabella Stewart Gardner Museum heist remains the largest such crime in world history, a brazen theft that still has investigators and law enforcement across the globe scratching their heads.

SOMEONE'S AT THE DOOR

In 2020, while America, along with the rest of the world, was distracted with riots, pandemics, and lockdowns, a meeting was held in the relatively obscure town of Davos, Switzerland. There, world leaders from ninety-one countries, including fifty-three heads of state, along with some of the world's most influential bankers and financiers, convened for a pivotal summit. These are considered to be the global elites, a veritable who's who of internationally known, powerful, geopolitical celebrities. But this was not the first such assembly. For forty-eight previous years, the same organization had been sponsoring this event.

The World Economic Forum (WEF) was founded in 1971 by Klaus Schwab, a German engineer and economist and a former professor of business policy at the University of Geneva. The organization's stated mission is to "shape global, regional, and industry agendas."[1] Like the aforementioned impostor policemen, their intentions are anything but honorable. Instead, they are standing at the door, armed with a clear and radical vision for Earth and its inhabitants.

Among the attendees at the 2020 summit were Prince Charles of Wales; Ursula von der Leyen (president of the European Commission); Christine Lagarde (president, European Central Bank); Seth F. Berkley (CEO of the Global Alliance for Vaccines and Immunizations); "His All-Holiness" Ecumenical Patriarch Bartholomew (the archbishop of Constantinople–New Rome); and, of course, Klaus Schwab (the founder of the nefarious organization). Also tagging along as a featured speaker was Earth's favorite teenage wannabe climate expert, Greta Thunberg. President Joe Biden of the United States was the keynote speaker at this conference in 2016, having also attended nine previous years.

But what were they doing there?

The Davos 2020 agenda was themed "Stakeholders for a Cohesive and Sustainable World," with a focus on "renewing the concept of stakeholder capitalism to overcome income inequality, societal division and the climate crisis."[2]

However, the January 2020 agenda turned out to be merely the warm-up act for what was to come. In June of that same year, Schwab released a book titled *COVID-19: The Great Reset*. In it he outlines a proposed plan for leveraging the COVID-19 crisis as a way to address everything from climate change to world economics, human equality, and, of course, pandemics. According to Schwab, "the pandemic represents a rare but narrow window of opportunity to reflect, reimagine, and reset our world."[3]

Schwab's strategy for the planet, as outlined in his book (and representing the official global strategy of the WEF), proposes passing over a threshold that has never before been crossed—and toward a point of no return. The whole idea of a global reset is predicated upon planetary unity between nations. Under a new umbrella of "equality," individualism and nationalism are portrayed as the enemies. In fact, Schwab describes nationalism as nothing more than the history of nations conquering oppressed peoples. Under globalism, one surrenders all of one's "privilege"—whether it be from one's race, gender, or national affiliation. World peace, another element in the plan, is achieved when religious intolerance is erased. There are no borders in this new world of globalism. This philosophy is on full display through President Joe Biden's porous border policy, as the commander in chief has effectively dismantled Donald Trump's attempts at securing America's boundaries.[4] Unfortunately, this illegal immigration crisis is not likely to be solved. With globalism, there is also no segmenting between citizens and noncitizens, as we are all *world citizens*. Those who oppose this growing surge of globalism are perceived as hindrances to progress and peace in the human race. The ideology of a "global environment" is what unites us now, and a one-world government is the ultimate goal. Slogans such as "America First" are labeled as elitist, arrogant, and even a form of white nationalism. But though it is marketed as a sort of "new capitalism," globalism is actually the antithesis, as it seeks to flatten the curve financially, directly threatening capitalism and a free society—and life as we know it.

Because of imposed COVID-19 restrictions, the January 2021 Davos Conference was held virtually.

Much like the coronavirus, the WEF also began rather stealthily. Fifty years ago, Schwab founded the nonprofit under the name European Management Forum. Since that time, in a spirit of unapologetic hypocrisy, these global one-percenters have flown from all over the world on private jets to import wisdom on how to save the planet from fossil fuel emissions and climate change.

According to founder Schwab, among the chief goals of the WEF is to create a "cohesive and sustainable world."[5] The 2021 gathering was their most relevant to date, as the current global health crisis provided a golden opportunity to accelerate those goals. That year's agenda included more fully defining the term "stakeholder capitalism," a phrase used by the WEF and its founder to refer to a new model of doing world business, one where "people and the planet" are the focus. In Schwab's own words, "the planet is thus the center of the global economic system, and its health should be optimized in the decisions made by all the other stakeholders" (general public).[6]

Put more plainly, "We the People" now exist to serve the planet and to work for the collective good of all. This effectively translates into old-fashioned socialism. Phrases like "global equity" and "consumption inequality," though perhaps noble sounding, are laced with an emotional narcotic meant to dull the mind to the WEF's real agenda: to transform free people into servants of government—and to globalism itself.

Ownership of material goods in their new world agenda is frowned upon. In its place, citizens are expected to more responsibly consume services that are provided to them by companies and governments. And for their part, companies should consider lowering their prices or even "ask themselves whether they could succeed if their product was free."[7]

"KNOCK, KNOCK"

The COVID-19 phenomenon that burst across the world in 2020 can only be described as cataclysmic, and some would say even "apocalyptic." Within weeks of the initial outbreak, governments across the globe were feeling the concentric ripple effects of the growing pandemic. Like islanders hunkering down before a tsunami, nations began bracing themselves for the impact of the ever-widening swath of sickness associated with such devastating plagues. The ensuing dread evoked historical fears dating from the bubonic plague to the 1918 influenza, which killed up to one hundred million people. In short, the COVID-19 epidemic whipped the world into a fear-fueled frenzy. Based on initial forecasts, a common belief was that hospitals would be filled to overflowing and unable to treat the vast numbers of patients brought to their doors. Makeshift triage units were hastily put together as the volume of cases was expected to exponentially explode in the days ahead.

President Donald Trump even sent the USNS *Comfort*, a

Navy hospital ship, to New York City harbor in an effort to provide added relief to a projected overstressed hospital system.

However, as it turned out, the virus's eventual impact proved much weaker than those initial forecasts. The *New York Times* reported at the outset that we could see well over two million deaths from COVID-19 in the United States alone, while experts were in consensus that the mortality rate was only 0.9 percent, or less than 1 percent.[8] Mental images of dead bodies stacked ten high in the streets were soon replaced by more realistic scenarios. Even so, lockdowns, quarantines, and mask wearing quickly became the norm. The *Comfort* was sent home after treating fewer than two hundred cases, and the number of actual COVID-19 deaths or COVID-19-related deaths never reached anywhere near early predictions. In fact, according to the Centers for Disease Control and Prevention (CDC), by August 2020, 94 percent of patients who at that time reportedly died from coronavirus also had other "health conditions and contributing [comorbidity] causes."[9] In other words, only 6 percent of reported deaths were due to COVID-19 alone.

Even so, Pandora's box had been opened.

Though the actual death rates were much less than originally feared, the impact of the COVID-19 pandemic nevertheless proved to be immeasurable in both its depth and scope. Who could have imagined that a tiny, invisible virus could have escaped from a Chinese laboratory, only to cripple economies, lock down billions, and reportedly kill millions? But with the virus also came other unintended side effects. What few saw coming were the ways governments worldwide became engorged with a sudden increase of power and control. In an effort to bring calm in the midst of chaos, national and local leaders imposed restrictive mandates on the populace. Self-regulation was quickly replaced with mandatory governmental guidelines. And compliance was compulsory. Lockdowns and the isolation of millions of healthy citizens replaced concerts, church gatherings, and football games. Freedoms were curtailed and fines introduced, with arrest and imprisonment threatened against those who failed to comply. Entire countries effectively shut down. Millions of jobs were lost or suspended, some never to be regained. Thousands of businesses were forced to close their doors. And in spite of welcomed government stimulus checks, the economy sputtered to restart. Over a billion children worldwide were suddenly out of school and at home. And with families confined to their homes for extended periods, mental health experts feared an uptick in domestic abuse, depression, and suicide. Unfortunately, their fears were realized, as a dramatic increase in suicide rates swept across the nation. In California, doctors reported more deaths from suicide than from the coronavirus, seeing "a year's worth of suicides in just four weeks." And in one county in Tennessee, "more people died of suicide than in the entire state directly from the virus."[10] Clearly, both individuals and countries struggled to endure and manage this global train wreck.

COVID-19 was like a sudden unforeseen storm out of nowhere, blindsiding us all. Reeling from the impact, we still did what we could to somehow put our lives back together again. Meanwhile, in the midst of the confusing chaos caused by the pandemic, another agenda was being discussed.

THE DAVOS DECEPTION

Because the elite who make up the WEF believe we are a planet in perilous transition, they continue frantically spinning the

COVID-19 crisis to their advantage. They do not hide the fact that the globalism they propose is rooted in democratic socialism and world citizenship. That in itself is alarming enough, as the socialist experiment has been a dismal failure in every country where it has been applied. History records that the degree of economic disaster and human genocide left in its wake is almost incalculable.

In the minds of globalists, world history is the tragic tale of endless conflicts in wars between independent tribes and nations. Religion and political persuasions are painted as servants of evil empires whose only goal is to separate, segregate, and dominate. Therefore, they feel compelled to break down the ideological barriers that prevent the rule of equality and ensure "justice for all."

As a result, a huge component of this radical ideological shift necessitates a "geopolitical reset," meaning that nationalism (nations governing themselves independently) must be replaced by a global governance system where services, people, capital, and data can be freely exchanged. This is the basic concept of world citizenry, and the European Commission (a politically independent executive branch of the European Union) is the most famous trial run at implementing this ideology among nations.

So globalism becomes the foundation of world citizenry, and individualism must yield to the collective whole. This effectively means the dissolution of borders. No national allegiances. And no patriotism. What unites this new world is the eradication of long-held capitalistic ventures and pursuits. In their place, a socialist, more equitable (and godless) commitment to the earth's government, and to the earth itself. Father God is officially replaced with Mother Nature. Socialism replaces national sovereignty. Slogans like "God Bless America" are not only cast into the ash heap of history but also branded as outdated, shameful, and even evil. With capitalism and a free society, there are winners and losers—those who succeed and those who fail. The rich and the poor. But under globalism, all people are "equal," and wealth is redistributed fairly among the masses (at least in theory).

Under globalism, citizens are forcibly transformed from *shareholders* (with something to gain) into *stakeholders* (with something to "contribute to the world"). Schwab, as the undisputed godfather of globalism, has drafted a manifesto for this coming new reality, one that outlines a "path that will take us to a better world: one which is more inclusive, more equitable, and more respectful of Mother Nature."[11] By "more inclusive," he means, in part, no more economic borders. By "more equitable," he means leveling the playing field between the rich and the rest of us. And by "more respectful of Mother Nature," he means taxing citizens into oblivion if they consume the earth's resources (gas, oil, electricity), which, in turn, promotes a more climate-friendly existence. Under a globalist regime, the collective well-being of the planet and its people takes precedence over gross domestic product growth. Essentially, one's personal energy and economics now exist for the good of others and not just oneself.

Since 1971 Schwab and his fellow earth-shaping comrades have convened each year to brainstorm concerning how to overtake existing national infrastructures and turn them into spokes in a global wheel, which feeds into a unified central world government. The self-labeled "Davos Agenda" is an integral part of his vision to "reimagine our world."[12] Quoting a Singaporean diplomat, he and his coauthor, Thierry Malleret, liken the seven-plus billion people on planet Earth not to those who inhabit "one hundred separate boats [countries]" but rather to people living in "193 cabins on the same boat."[13] Therefore, if the boat we are all on suddenly contracts a virus (think COVID-19), we should not selfishly be concerned with our own cabins (countries) but also the corridors through which the virus travels (i.e., other countries and the whole world).

The globalist leader rightly connects the dots between infectious pandemics and global governance failures, social instability, and fiscal crises. The Bible prophesied such connected phenomenon two thousand years ago (Revelation 6:1–8). He also links the potential domino effects of other ripple-causing events—such as natural disasters, human-made environmental disasters, state collapses, national financial failures, and widespread cyberattacks. In light of these realities, globalists like Schwab are intentional about accelerating their one-world agenda before the clock strikes midnight and a mass extinction event threatens the planet. From Schwab's perspective, he has good reason to do so. As of 2021, the official "Doomsday Clock" was set to "100 seconds to midnight," meaning the existential threat to humanity on a global scale is closer now than it has ever been in human history.[14]

The bottom line is that the world must come together, and *right now*. To do this, the planet must reboot. Hence, a global *reset*.

Fortuitously, the COVID-19 crisis turned out to be a gift for the globalists, opening the door for nations across the world to lay aside their differences in order to form alliances for the greater good of the world and its people. "Global governance" is exactly what it sounds like. Nations become "nation-states," subsisting under the umbrella of a centralized authority. Their agenda promises to fundamentally change the world and the way it operates, much like when former president Barack Obama pledged to fundamentally change America. What truly saddens the WEF is that they presently live in a world in which "nobody is really in charge."[15] In their worldview, nations are essentially seen as children who simply cannot govern themselves or get along with one another. Therefore, what is needed is an authority figure, or "parent," an entity whose role is to regulate and direct them. That authority would be this centralized world government. By their own admission, the United Nations is impotent, the World Health Organization is underfunded, and the European Commission is ineffective in sufficiently filling the present vacuum of leadership.

We must, therefore, "reset."

However, there are obstacles in their path, one of the largest having been former president Donald Trump and his administration, who stood squarely in the way of this progress. To move forward with their agenda, Trump needed to be removed from power.

BIG BROTHER IS WATCHING

Another essential component of this globalist agenda is harvesting and maintaining the constant gathering of information from individuals. To keep a society healthy from pandemics like COVID-19, for example, the government must mine data from its citizens in order to know who has been sick, who is infected, and the whereabouts of those who have been exposed to such viruses.

Technologies like contact tracing and tracking are thus justified and employed. Schwab and Malleret write:

> Contact tracing and tracking are both terms used interchangeably, yet they have slightly different meanings. A tracking app gains insights in real time by, for example, determining a person's current location through geo-data via GPS coordinates or radio cell location. By contrast, tracing consists in gaining insight in retrospect, like identifying physical contact between people using Bluetooth.[16]

However, they also admit that the same type of tracing could be implemented digitally under different forms. For example, countries like China and South Korea have used more "coercive and intrusive measures of digital tracing."[17] They have tracked individuals without their consent through their mobile phones and credit card data, and even used video surveillance on them. In Hong Kong some individuals have been forced to wear electronic bracelets when arriving in the country so that they could be monitored and tracked and also to alert individuals around them that they may be susceptible to being infected. Schwab and Malleret admit that this technology could be used in the name of public health for "political means and more sinister ends."[18]

But it does not necessarily stop there. Historian Yuval Noah Harari penned an article imagining what this totalitarian surveillance could look like. He writes:

> Consider a hypothetical government that demands that every citizen wears a biometric bracelet that monitors body

temperature and heart-rate 24 hours a day. The resulting data is hoarded and analyzed by government algorithms. The algorithms will know that you are sick even before you know it, and they will also know where you have been, and who you have met. The chains of infection could be drastically shortened, and even cut altogether. Such a system could arguably stop the epidemic in its tracks within days. Sounds wonderful, right?

The downside is, of course, that this would give legitimacy to a terrifying new surveillance system. If you know, for example, that I clicked on a Fox News link rather than a CNN link, that can teach you something about my political views and perhaps even my personality. But if you can monitor what happens to my body temperature, blood pressure and heart-rate as I watch the video clip, you can learn what makes me laugh, what makes me cry, and what makes me really, really angry.

... The same technology that identifies coughs could also identify laughs. If corporations and governments start harvesting our barometric data en masse, they can get to know us far better than we know ourselves, and they can then not just predict our feelings but also manipulate our feelings and sell us anything they want—be it a product or a politician. Biometric monitoring would make Cambridge Analytica's data hacking tactics look like something from the Stone Age. Imagine North Korea in 2030, when every citizen has to wear a biometric bracelet 24 hours a day. If you listen to a speech by the Great Leader and the bracelet picks up the tell-tale signs of anger, you are done for.[19]

Should a crisis be severe enough (i.e., another global pandemic), such monitoring in some form could be justified in the name of public health, personal safety, or responsible citizenship. Of course, we are not there yet, and the WEF is not currently advocating such surveillance. But if the right (evil) person occupied the primary seat in a future global government, this type of control technology could be a potential option.

Schwab and his WEF cohorts from around the world are unequivocally advocating for this great reset, about which he boldly asserts, "Without delay, we need to set [it] in motion," adding that it is an "absolute necessity."[20] President Joe Biden ran for office under the slogan, "Build Back Better," a catchphrase taken directly from the WEF's globalist playbook.[21]

With COVID-19 the narrative of fear and death gained traction. The planet bought into mask mandates and submitted to lockdowns, social distancing, and sheltering at home, and in doing so relinquished control of their way of life. On the heels of these restrictions, the introductions of various vaccines began rolling into communities like ice cream trucks in a neighborhood full of kids. Millions lined up to be injected with what amounted to be experimental drugs that failed to provide actual immunity after all, only helping mask COVID-19's symptoms.[22] Children were targeted next, with the CDC recommending the jab for kids as young as five.[23] In Israel, where nearly 80 percent of the population received the shot, COVID-19 cases nevertheless surged among the vaccinated.[24]

This overall crisis was the open door the WEF had waited for. In order to fix the planet, it was concluded, they would first have to *remake* it. And that would mean seizing the moment and making their move. They are not finished. What is at stake here is much more valuable than a gallery full of priceless art. It is more like a universal heist. A *global reset*.

In other words, they are at the door and plan to steal the *world*.

RETURN TO BABYLON

These realities are alarming by themselves. And yet there remains a deeper, more sinister agenda embedded within. According to prophecies found in the Bible, a one-world government will indeed emerge in the end times. To more fully understand this coming kingdom, we have to grasp how both Daniel and Revelation describe it. In Daniel 2, King Nebuchadnezzar had a dream where he saw a very large statue made of gold, silver, bronze, iron, and clay. Each of these metals, we discover, represents world kingdoms corresponding to Babylon, Medo-Persia, Greece, and Rome. Then, in chapter 7, Daniel had his own dream-vision concerning these same empires, only they were portrayed not as components of a statue, but rather as four ravenous beasts—a lion, a bear, a leopard, and a fourth beast described as "dreadful and terrifying and extremely strong" (Daniel 7:7). This beast had iron teeth and crushed and trampled down its opponents. It is also described as "different from all the beasts that were before it," having "ten horns" (7:7).

The angel later explained to Daniel that these ten horns represent "ten kings" who rule over their own kingdoms (7:24; see also Revelation 13:1; 17:12). However, what is important to note here is that historically Rome never actually existed in a ten-kingdom conglomerate. Therefore, we can safely conclude that this expression of the Roman Empire must be in the future.

In other words, Scripture predicts a Revived Roman Empire that will arise in the last days. Rome 2.0, if you will.

The apostle John confirmed this same formation of an end-times world kingdom. "And the dragon stood on the sand of the seashore. Then I saw a beast coming up out of the sea, having ten horns and seven heads, and on his horns were ten diadems, and on his heads were blasphemous names" (Revelation 13:1).

Concerning the seven heads, they were later revealed to signify seven successive world regimes: Egypt, Assyria, Babylon, Medo-Persia, Greece, Rome, and the kingdom led by the Antichrist—namely, a Revived Roman Empire (Revelation 17:9–10). The angel giving John this apocalyptic revelation specifically explained, "The ten horns which you saw are ten kings who have not yet received a kingdom, but they receive authority as kings with the beast for one hour. These have one purpose, and they give their power and authority to the beast" (vv. 12–13). Just a few verses later, John was told that this one-world, unified kingdom is a part of God's sovereign, prophetic plan. "For God has put it in their hearts to execute His purpose by having a common purpose, and by giving their kingdom to the beast, until the words of God will be fulfilled" (v. 17). This not only tells us how sovereign God is but also how specifically every one of these future prophecies will come to pass (Job 42:2; Matthew 5:17–18; 24:34–35; Revelation 4:1).

According to Revelation 13:3, 7, this future unified government will encompass the whole earth. It will directly be energized by Satan for the ultimate purpose of ruling over all the earth and being worshiped by its inhabitants (Revelation 13:12, 15–16). This, Scripture tells us, has been the devil's ambition since the day he aspired to overthrow heaven (Isaiah 14:12–15; Ezekiel 28:11–19).

What is significant, however, about this coming one-world government is that current global conditions appear to be harbingers for its (perhaps) soon appearance. Like dominoes, one significant earthshaking occurrence leads to the next . . . and to the next. Though humanity has seen multiple attempts in the last hundred years to achieve global cooperation and world peace—the League of Nations in 1919, the United Nations in 1945, the European Union in 1958, and the WEF in 1971—none has succeeded. And Scripture's Revived Roman Empire has yet to materialize. Interestingly, when the European Union was founded, representatives from six nations (Belgium, France, Italy, Luxembourg, the Netherlands, and West Germany) convened on Capitoline Hill, the site of multiple temples to an array of pagan gods. It was there they inked the deal on a historic document, aptly named, the Treaty of Rome.[25]

Other multinational gatherings and summits have followed, but none so intentional as the recent agenda of the WEF. This is not to suggest that the WEF is the fulfillment of Daniel's prophetic vision. There is no way to definitively know this at our present place in God's prophetic timetable. However, it is to say that the *spirit* of their agenda undoubtably dovetails rather seamlessly with the future empire predicted in Scripture. As we (hopefully) exit the tunnel of the planetwide COVID-19 crisis, this recent push for global convergence is the most significant prophetic foreshadowing of what is to come.

The prophecies made by Daniel and John appear to be coming together at an accelerated rate, faster than at any time in modern memory. In short, never has the idea of a one-world government been as palatable to the international community as it is *right now*. And that should get our attention.

Two years before the now-famous Isabella Stewart Gardner Museum art heist, its board of directors were told that the Federal Bureau of Investigation (FBI) had foiled a plan by thieves to rob the museum. Urged to invest in theft insurance, they refused, perhaps because the $3 million policy was greater than their annual operating budget. Or they may have concluded that, were they to be robbed, no amount of money would be able to replace the priceless works of art housed there. Whatever the case, following the heist, not a penny was ever claimed or awarded to them. Today if you visit the museum, you will see empty frames once graced by glorious masterpieces. And by every indication, those works will likely never be recovered. They were stolen and are lost to history.

The Bible prophesies the inevitable capitulation of nations and their convergence into a global governing body during the last days. This act will bring about the fulfillment of many other ancient apocalyptic prophecies. And just like a grand heist, it will catch most of the world by surprise, leaving an empty void where sovereign nations once stood.

TWO

SURGING GLOBAL DELUSION

Not long ago, my (Jeff) wife and I attended a concert by a well-known artist. Prior to his performance, however, an opening act took the stage. Much to the crowd's delight, this man turned out to be an award-winning illusionist. Immaculately dressed in a theatrical black suit, his wide smile and brilliant white teeth seemed to illuminate the venue. He began predictably enough, with a few sleight-of-hand tricks that warmed up the audience. Each trick was followed by polite applause. However, as the presentation continued, the Vegas-style performer progressively transitioned to more complicated and impressive illusions. All this "theater" was meant to prepare us for his grand finale. The curtain behind him parted, revealing, to our amazement, a full-size helicopter parked on the stage. Of course, everyone suspected what was about to happen. The illusionist and his lovely assistants began their well-dressed choreography leading up to the evening's magical magnum opus. Another smaller curtain was wheeled onto center stage, momentarily obscuring the helicopter.

More smiles and choreographed dance moves followed, accompanied by background music, which only heightened the tension of the moment. Then, at the appointed time, the music crescendoed, then abruptly halted. A pregnant pause silenced the theater. Then the smiling man in the suit suddenly broke his grin, trading it for a more serious countenance. With an ultradramatic sweeping hand wave, the curtain dropped, revealing an empty stage behind it. A collective gasp swept across the packed audience, turning almost immediately into thunderous applause. The illusionist acknowledged our wonder and strutted forward to center stage to take a bow, and then another, prompting the thousand or so in attendance there that evening to stand for an extended ovation. As he proudly exited stage left, the mind of every person in the audience entertained the same question: "How in the world did he do that?"

Our eyes were telling us one thing but our minds another. While we knew intellectually that a man cannot make a helicopter disappear, our eyes bore testimony to a different story, and reality. We knew it was not real; nevertheless, a part of us still believed it.

And that is precisely why they call it an "illusion."

BIGGER STAGE, BIGGER ILLUSION

The Bible tells us a day is coming when someone much more convincing than a magician will appear upon the world's stage. It is he who will fully accomplish a *global reset*. One man, accompanied by his assistant, will succeed in misleading billions, thoroughly persuading them regarding an alternate reality. That man is called by many names in Scripture, but you know him best as the Antichrist (Matthew 24:5; 1 John 2:18, 22; 4:3; 2 John v. 7).

Daniel described this enigmatic man as a person of unparalleled cunning and deceit.

> A king will arise,
> Insolent and skilled in intrigue.
> His power will be mighty, but not by his own
>   power,
> And he will destroy to an extraordinary degree
> And prosper and perform his will;
> He will destroy mighty men and the holy people.
> And through his shrewdness
> He will cause deceit to succeed by his influence;
> And he will magnify himself in his heart,
> And he will destroy many while they are at ease.
> He will even oppose the Prince of princes,
> But he will be broken without human agency.
>   (Daniel 8:23–25)

This particular prophetic passage, like others, has both a near and far fulfillment. It would first apply to Antiochus Epiphanes, a ruler in the Seleucid dynasty who murdered his way to the throne. Antiochus attacked Jerusalem in 167 BC in an attempt to destroy the Jewish people. He embodied a unique blend of evil and ego, mixed with disdain for the Jewish people and spelling disaster for them. After conquering Jerusalem, Antiochus entered the temple, whereupon he slaughtered a pig on the altar as an offering to Zeus, a brazen mockery to both Israel and their God. The name

Epiphanes means "God manifest." However, the Jews altered it, referring to him as Epimanes, meaning "madman."

But Daniel's prophecy has a future fulfillment as well, and it is found in Scripture's son of destruction (2 Thessalonians 2:3). While Antiochus has been called the "Old Testament Antichrist," the man portrayed in the rest of Daniel and Revelation is the real deal—*the* Antichrist. He will be the ultimate man of sin. Deceit and trickery will be staples of his modus operandi. That's because wherever there is truth, Satan seeks to counterfeit it. To sell it as a "knockoff," a cleverly disguised and carefully cloaked forgery.

Fast-forwarding to the New Testament, Jesus also spoke of these future fake-faith peddlers. In the last instructions to his disciples regarding the end times, he warned, "See to it that no one misleads you. For many will come in My name, saying, 'I am the Christ,' and will mislead many" (Matthew 24:4–5).

He repeated a similar prophecy in verse 11: "Many false prophets will arise and lead many astray" (ESV). And again in verses 22–25, "Unless those days had been cut short, no life would have been saved; but for the sake of the elect those days will be cut short. Then if anyone says to you, 'Behold, here is the Christ,' or 'There He is,' do not believe him. For false Christs and false prophets will arise and will show great signs and wonders, so as to *mislead*, if possible, even the elect. Behold I have told you in advance" (emphasis added).

Christ's repeated warnings give us a clue as to the spiritual climate of the last days. Specifically, here Jesus was referring to the final seven-year period known as the tribulation. The Bible tells us those days will inaugurate an era of great deception and horror, the likes of which the world has never before seen or experienced (Matthew 24:21). But there is far more than trickery, misdirection, and sleight of hand going on here. The deception prevalent in those coming days goes deeper, and darker, than the innocence of a theater gathering. Paul, under the guidance of the Holy Spirit, put it this way:

> Then that lawless one will be revealed whom the Lord will slay with the breath of His mouth and bring to an end by the appearance of His coming; that is, the one whose coming is in accord with the activity of Satan, *with all power and signs and false wonders, and with all the deception of wickedness* for those who perish, because they did not receive the love of the truth so as to be saved. (2 Thessalonians 2:8–10, emphasis added)

Paul's prophecy tells us the end times will witness an explosion of supernatural wonders and delusion. Billions will be thoroughly convinced of Satan's lies told through the Antichrist, as they will be authenticated with amazing displays of miraculous deeds.

This principle of delusion is not a recent concept, as it was very active in the first century. In the years following the birth of the Christian church, Satan, called by Jesus the "father of lies" (John 8:44), was alive and well on planet Earth. His influence and agents infiltrated the body of Christ. In his epistles to the churches, Paul repeatedly addressed false teaching, impostor apostles, demonic doctrines, and subtle, deceptive beliefs and influences. In fact, most of his letters were written to refute heretical beliefs and apostate teachings. Had he not done so, the purity of the gospel would have suffered, and the churches would have been perpetually plagued by confusion, with members trusting in a bogus gospel and a counterfeit Christianity.

Satan's surging delusion has many tentacles. From Scripture we can identify four areas concerning how he works in our world today.

1. He Darkens Minds

Satan's primary agenda for the world, from the first century until now, remains the same—to prevent people from hearing and believing the gospel, and thus from being saved. That is because when salvation does occur, the individual is "rescued . . . from the [Satan's] domain of darkness, and transferred . . . to the kingdom of [God's] beloved Son" (Colossians 1:13). It is critical to keep in mind that the devil craves control and worship. These make up the fuel on which his kingdom runs. His ego is fed in part through the number of nations, governments, institutions, and individuals over which he can exercise authority and dominion. And by the look of things, business is currently good—very good.

Concerning how he prevents people from responding to the gospel, as the "god of this world," Satan blinds "the minds of the unbelieving so that they might not see the light of the gospel of the glory of Christ, who is the image of God" (2 Corinthians 4:4). His influence through this world system and through partnering with our own sin nature forms a spiritual barrier, keeping humankind from seeing and encountering the glorious light of the gospel of the glory of Christ (Romans 12:1–2; 1 John 2:15–17). As long as Satan can keep people in darkness (i.e., not hearing or comprehending God's truth), he knows they will continue stumbling and fumbling blindly about in life. This spiritual blindness cuts off all contact with the gospel. Thus, the devil does everything within his power to keep the lights turned off, lest people hear, see, and believe in Jesus, who said of himself, "I am the *Light* of the world; he who follows Me will not walk in the darkness, but will have the *Light of life*" (John 8:12, emphasis added).

2. He Distracts Desires

Like the consummate illusionist he is, the devil is the master of misdirection, diverting people's attention away from the truth and toward more temporal pursuits—jobs, money, career, romance, relationships, self-love, false religions, social issues, and empty philosophies.

If he can convince people they are not really that sinful before God, then they will not comprehend their desperate need for salvation through Christ. He leads them to believe that God will eventually welcome everyone to heaven, or at least that committing their lives to God is a decision they will be able to make at a much later date. This is part of what Jesus referenced in the parable of the sower and the soils: "The word is sown; and when they hear, immediately Satan comes and takes away the word which has been sown in them" (Mark 4:15).

Like a bird perched above in a tree, Satan swoops down to snatch up the freshly sown seed of God's truth before it has a chance to implant itself in them.

A second type of person, Jesus said, "immediately receive[s] it [the word] with joy; and they have no firm root in themselves, but are only temporary" (Mark 4:16–17). In almost forty years of ministry, I have observed that the "first responders" to Jesus, or those who exhibit the most enthusiasm at the beginning, are also those who are the first to fall away. In fact, the bigger their excitement, typically, the faster they fall. They show up, Bible in hand, sitting in the front row and filled with eagerness to learn. And yet, in a short time, they are easily taken out and taken away, sometimes by the simplest difficulty associated with their newly professed faith. And I never see them again. Just like Jesus said.

But Satan is not content simply to steal the seed or hope they will lose interest in the gospel. He also ensures there is a "backup plan" just in case the individual is entertaining God's truth. In which case, his strategy of *distraction* kicks in. "And others are the ones on whom seed was sown among the thorns; these are the ones who have heard the word, but the worries of the world, and the deceitfulness of riches, and the desires for other things enter in and choke the word, and it becomes unfruitful" (Mark 4:18–19).

Considering all that fills our lives today—family, jobs, school, hobbies, friendships, making money, the struggle for significance, the need to be liked or to feel important, along with other worldly pursuits—these "thorns" can easily become satanic tools used to divert our minds and desires from the one thing that really matters: our souls.

Currently, the average person spends more than two hours per day on social media and more than five hours a day checking his or her phone, up to sixty-three times daily.[1] More alarming is the fact that, according to a Barna study, in the past year, just 9 percent of Christians engaged in daily Bible reading.[2] This is down from an already dismal 14 percent. Apparently, not even believers have room for God in their schedules. Distractions.

3. He Deceives Hearts

A third strategy of Satan in the last days includes both subtle deception and blatant lies. And nothing could be truer to his character, as Scripture calls him "the deceiver of the whole world" (Revelation 12:9 ESV). This deception will dramatically ramp up in the earth's final days. Revelation 13 tells us the second "beast" of the tribulation (the false prophet) is granted power as he "deceives those who dwell on the earth" (v. 14). This man is working with, and directly underneath, the Antichrist. His role is to promote the first beast's agenda, and together with him and Satan, this diabolical trinity ignites a storm surge of deception across the entire planet.

Satan's diabolical desire to "deceive the nations" will continue until that moment when he is bound and cast into the abyss for a thousand years (Revelation 20:3). And yet even there his nature and desire remain fixed. After being placed in solitary confinement for a millennium, he will bolt from the darkness like a horse out of the gate, prepared to deceive the nations one last time (Revelation 20:7–8). This ought to highlight the damning danger of Satan's deceptions at work today. He is relentless and never runs out of ammunition in his attacks against us. He possesses an endless supply of flaming arrows (Ephesians 6:16), and many of them are dipped in deceit. When under the influence of this drug of deception, people are helpless and hopeless to see themselves, life, others, or God in any other way.

This is why Paul urged the Ephesian believers, "Put on the whole armor of God, that you may be able to stand against the schemes [lit., "cunning deceptions"] of the devil" (Ephesians 6:11 ESV). In fact, so refined are his masquerading skills that this prince of darkness "disguises himself as an angel of light" (2 Corinthians 11:14).[3] And because he can appear as an angel of light, only those with discerning hearts can spot the difference, not just between good and evil but also between truth mixed with lies (1 Corinthians 2:11, 15–16; Philippians 1:9; Hebrews 5:11–14).

So, if we who have the "mind of Christ" often have difficulty spotting Satan's deceptions (1 Corinthians 2:16), what chance do the unsaved of this world have? What discernment do they possess? They are essentially defenseless and, apart from the saving work of God, destined for continued deception. There is not a territory or a town on planet Earth today where this deception is not in operation.

Can you understand more fully now why John wrote, "The whole world lies in the power of the evil one" (1 John 5:19)?

4. He Dilutes Truth

A fourth way Satan is placing the world under a global delusion is by challenging, questioning, modifying, and reimagining the Word of God. This, in fact, was his first ever scheme used on the earth and is still one of his strongest and most effective weapons. With humanity still fresh on the scene, the garden serpent casually and stealthily approached Adam's wife, causing the newly crafted couple to question the clearly revealed truth God had just given them.

"Indeed, has God said . . . ?" (Genesis 3:1).

And with those four words, one of the world's most successful and efficient sales campaigns was launched. The Hebrew phrase here can also be translated "Is it true?" In other words, "Did God *really* say . . . ? Are you sure you heard him correctly?" So, the first recorded question in God's Word is one that questions God himself. Challenging the revealed Word of God is powerful because it creates doubt, not only about what he has said but also about his very character. Essentially, a God who would keep you from the Tree of Knowledge of Good and Evil must also be the kind of God who has something to hide. Indeed, he must be holding out on you, preventing you from experiencing all that the world, and life, has to offer. Therefore, how can he really be "good"? And therefore, how can he be trusted?

In these last days, there is no shortage of those who dispute, dilute, reinterpret, reimagine, rewrite, and outright deny God's Word.

From Genesis . . .

- Creation did not happen. The universe magically appeared out of nothing, and we evolved over millions of years.
- Creation did not happen the way the Bible claims. Seriously? That is impossible.
- Adam and Eve were not actual people but rather metaphorical representatives of the human race.
- Genesis cannot be a literal account of a six-day creation because "*science* says. . . ."

. . . to Revelation

- The events of Revelation already happened in the first century.
- Revelation is merely a book of symbols, not literal prophecies.
- Revelation is like the rest of the Bible, irrelevant and only for weak, superstitious religious people.
- Revelation should not be studied. No one could ever make sense of it.
- The rapture is not real.
- Jesus is not coming back . . . ever. *Period.*

We also see this thinking applied to virtually every topic and issue that really matters today:

- **Sexuality and Morality**—God's Word is obsolete, antiquated. Dismiss it or update it to accommodate moral fluidity.
- **Human Identity**—If you imagine or feel yourself to be another gender, then you are. Even though God's Word repeatedly and authoritatively states he "made them male and female" (Genesis 1:26–27; Matthew 19:4).
- **The Sanctity of Life**—It is a "clump of cells" and a "woman's right to choose," not a baby created in the image of God. Scripture tells a different story (Psalm 139:13–16; Jeremiah 1:5; Luke 1:15, 41).
- **The Future of Planet Earth**—We make our own future and reality. Bible prophecy is a hoax. But according to Revelation 1:3, 19, it is anything but a hoax.

We even see this diluting of the Word in the church, where key doctrines are being reinterpreted for a new generation, and a growing apostasy is being unleashed in many major denominations, just as Paul prophesied concerning the last days (2 Thessalonians 2:3; 1 Timothy 4:1; 2 Timothy 4:3–4). We see it with morality being redefined in order to allow certain sexual lifestyles to be welcomed into the body of Christ. Even into the role of pastor. We see it with millennial Christians now "deconstructing" their faith and calling themselves "exvangelicals."[4]

And Satan's refrain is sung again: "Indeed, has God said . . . ?" (Genesis 3:1)

Can you hear this spirit reverberating on the airwaves, in the classrooms, on social media, in today's marketplace, and on Main

Street? Do you hear the serpent's voice whispering, "The bottom line, of course, in all this is that if God's Word cannot be trusted in matters of history and science, then why would we trust it in areas of spirituality, morality, and prophecy? And if it cannot be relied upon, then how can God himself be trusted? How can one even know that he is, what he is like, and what, if anything, he wants from us? Therefore, it is best not to trust his Word but rather your own heart."

Can you now see how diluting even one sentence of truth in God's Word undermines the entire foundation of our faith? The devil is right about one thing—if God's Word cannot be trusted in one place, then it cannot be trusted in any place. If Genesis did not get it right, what makes you think Revelation does? And yet David boldly declared:

> The law of the LORD is *perfect*, restoring the soul;
> The testimony of the LORD is *sure*, making wise
>   the simple.
> The precepts of the LORD are *right*, rejoicing the
>   heart;
> The commandment of the LORD is *pure*,
>   enlightening the eyes. (Psalm 19:7–8,
>   emphasis added)

Solomon, the wisest man in history, stated that "every word of God proves *true*" (Proverbs 30:5 ESV, emphasis added).

Jesus claimed that every single word and letter of Scripture will be proven true and trustworthy. "For truly I say to you, until heaven and earth pass away, not the smallest letter or stroke shall pass away from the Law until all is accomplished" (Matthew

5:18). He also claimed that his words are so true and reliable that they would outlast both heaven and earth (Matthew 24:35; Luke 16:17).

Paul asserted that *all* Scripture was directly from God and profitable for life (2 Timothy 3:16–17). Peter added that it contains everything we really need for life and godliness (2 Peter 1:3).

In response to Satan, these witnesses assert that, yes, God *has* said. And his Word *is* true.

The antidote to this diluting of the Word and for all of his deceptions is simply the Word itself, found in only one place—the Bible. If you want to recognize the subtleties of a counterfeit, then study the real thing.

Even so, Satan has no plans to surrender his long war against God and his Word. But even more in these last days, he will argue globally that God and his truth simply are not "enough." Humanity needs something more. Something else. Something *better*.

Something more real and convincing.

And like an eager salesman, Satan proposes, "And I've got just what you've been looking for."

THE AMAZING ANTICHRIST

Presently held back by the Holy Spirit's restraining influence through the church and her presence on the earth, Satan's "man of lawlessness" will eventually be given free rein to deceive the whole world (2 Thessalonians 2:6–8). But precisely how will he accomplish this grand deception? What will be his methods? What tools will he use?

Paul explained that the Antichrist's coming "is in accord with the activity of Satan, with all power and signs and false wonders, and with all the deception of wickedness for those who perish" (2 Thessalonians 2:9–10). There are several important truths we can learn from this passage.

First, the source of the Antichrist's authority is Satan himself. In Revelation 13 we are told that the "beast" receives his power directly from the "dragon" (Satan) and that his throne (rule) will be granted "great authority" (vv. 2, 4). The scope of this authority will extend over "every tribe and people and language and nation" (Revelation 13:7 ESV) and that "all who dwell on the earth will worship him" (Revelation 13:8).[5] That is a difficult concept to absorb, given that we have never experienced anything of this nature in our lifetime.

Second, the devil equips this man (and his false prophet) with the full arsenal of satanic power, including "signs and false wonders." Whatever resources are at Satan's disposal, the Antichrist will have access to them. An inexhaustible arsenal. So, will the Antichrist have the ability to perform actual supernatural signs and miracles, or will they simply be the most cleverly disguised illusions in human history?

A clue may be found in the original Greek words in this verse, where Paul used the same terms for "signs" and "wonders" that are used elsewhere in the New Testament to describe the miracles Jesus performed. This would lend credibility to the claim that these acts will be equal to the miracles done by the Lord during his earthly ministry. A further biblical clue is found in Paul's use of the word "false." The word could signify that they are not genuine supernatural occurrences or perhaps that they refer more to the *purpose* of such miracles (i.e., to mislead by propagating the Antichrist's deceptive agenda).

Remember that this beast is a *false* Christ, meaning he is convincing but still a counterfeit. The word *anti* means "in place of," as well as "against." These miracles and deceptions will be so real that, if allowed to continue, they would deceive even God's "elect"—if that were actually possible, which it is not (Matthew 24:24).

Concerning Paul's use of the word "false," Bible commentator William Hendriksen wrote, "But all of this display (powers, signs, and wonders) will spring from falsehood, from the desire to deceive."[6]

Are they "fake wonders," or real miracles that lead to a false conclusion, supporting the Antichrist's lying claims? D. Edmond Hiebert added, "It (the word 'false') does not assert that the miracles will be fraudulent, the result of trickery and pretense, but that they belong to the realm of falsehoods, faults and their very character."[7]

While Satan is a finite, limited being, there is some evidence that these miracles may indeed be actual and not merely an elaborate illusion. First, as an angel, the devil is a supernatural being. As such, he possesses the ability to operate outside the natural realm. In Scripture angels took on human form and exhibited many types of human behavior (Genesis 6:1–4; 19:1–22). These were not apparitions but by all indications flesh-and-blood men. Further, the magi of Egypt in Moses' day were able to perform supernatural acts using their "secret arts," most likely due to a connection to demonic powers (Exodus 7:11). Jesus prophesied that in the end times false prophets will appear and perform "great signs and wonders to deceive" (Matthew 24:24 NKJV). In the Old Testament, Satan was also endowed with the power to perform such miracles as calling down fire from heaven (Job 1:16) and controlling the wind (Job 1:19).

Second, during the tribulation (particularly the last three and a half years), Satan will be granted extended freedom in his effort to accomplish his long-sought agenda of ruling the world. In fact, the entire tribulation era will witness the return of supernatural occurrences, including not only the Antichrist's signs and wonders but also terrible apocalyptic judgments from God as well (Revelation 6–19).

So, it would appear that God, in his sovereignty, will lengthen the devil's leash during this time, allowing him to maximize his power to perform miraculous deeds. This combination of deception and the supernatural will prove to be a powerful cocktail, numbing the minds, hearts, and consciences of humanity. Satan's endgame, or purpose in all this, is to deceive the world into believing in his Antichrist and submitting to his world regime. Paul called this "the deception of wickedness for those who [will eventually] perish" (2 Thessalonians 2:10). And the resulting spiritual and geopolitical reset will indeed be *global*.

All this is made even more incredible when we consider how technologically savvy our world has become. Today, we hardly blink at the advancements we enjoy on a daily basis. In fact, it is hard to keep up with our rapidly changing technological landscape. Just last year, Amazon released a biometric scanning device called Amazon One. This machine can accurately read and scan your palm print, subdermal vein patterns, and even your bone structure perfectly, and it does that in 300 milliseconds. Heart transplants and brain surgery are commonplace. We have split the atom, gone to the moon several times, and are now planning trips to Mars. So, what's next? Fortunately, the Bible tells us that the day is rapidly approaching when human eyes once again will grow wider with wonder and mouths will drop open in amazement. The Antichrist and his false prophet will perform far greater wonders than Amazon, Apple, or NASA. In that era, humankind will witness supernatural signs in the sky and on the earth (Revelation 6–19), fire descending from heaven (13:13), inanimate objects coming to life (v. 15), and even a man brought back from the dead (v. 3)! The age of open, observable miracles will have returned.

Yes, Satan will deceive. And they will believe.

And yet, according to Scripture, a still worse fate awaits those who fall prey to his deceptions.

THREE

ONE WORLD UNDER THE ANTICHRIST

Frank Abagnale is considered to be one of the greatest con artists of all time. In the 1960s, while still a teenager, Abagnale began writing bogus checks. Not long afterward, he successfully posed as an airline pilot, sitting in the deadhead seat for various airlines in over 250 flights. He forged IDs and for a short while posed as a resident pediatrician at a Georgia hospital. He doctored a Harvard University law transcript and was somehow even able to pass the Louisiana bar exam.

Eventually, authorities caught up with him, and he was arrested in France in 1969. He spent time in a series of European prisons until finally being deported to the United States. However, en route, he managed to escape from one of the airplanes, fleeing through New York to Canada. There, while standing in line at a Canadian airport, he was spotted by a policeman and arrested. Imprisoned for several years, Abagnale was finally released in 1974, and after fumbling through a series of dead-end jobs, he eventually founded a consulting firm that advises companies concerning issues of fraud. He even taught at the FBI Academy and at Google headquarters. A movie was later made about his life, called *Catch Me If You Can*, starring Leonardo DiCaprio.

There are those who, in recent years, have doubted some of Abagnale's more outlandish claims and exploits. However, the fact that he fooled so many for so long only lends more credence to his effectiveness as a master impostor.

Frank Abagnale was a fraud. A forged persona, a charlatan, counterfeit, and deceiver.

But he is not the best.

Scripture tells us of another, much more sinister impostor. This evil entity flies under the radar and is rarely detected. Not content to merely mask himself, he also disguises his lies and schemes under false names and pseudonyms. And perhaps most deceptive of all, he kidnaps truth, goodness, and godly virtues, redefining and repurposing them for his own wicked agenda.

Here are some of them:

- *Truth* is no longer objective and absolute but rather more of an *idea* that morphs from person to person. Consequently, *my* truth may not be your truth, and vice versa.
- *Justice* is determined by societal perception, not an unchanging, impartial moral standard.
- *Equality* means everyone is guaranteed the same *outcome*. Equal opportunity in a free society is not enough. There must be assured equal success for all.

- *Hate* is redefined as "someone disagreeing with you."
- *Tolerance* means all beliefs and lifestyles are accepted and celebrated—except, of course, the beliefs of those who disagree with leftist, immoral values.
- *Freedom* means having the right to kill the baby in your womb if you do not want it. This is also called "health care" and "reproductive choice."
- *Gender* is no longer biological and determined at conception but is instead interchangeable, and a person is encouraged and empowered to totally redefine it through their thoughts and feelings.
- *Heaven* is everyone's birthright (should they choose to believe in such a thing), and God will eventually let everyone in.
- *Forgiveness* is for the weak and foolish. If you have said or done any single thing in your life that contradicts the present social and moral narrative, you will be summarily "canceled" and tossed into the forgotten files of history.
- *Love* is . . . well, *love*. Anyone is free to (romantically, sexually) love anyone else, regardless of age, gender, or orientation.
- *God* is whomever you imagine him (or her) to be.

We are living in an age when everything, including reality itself, is being redefined in order to conform to a godless worldview and its value system. But as far reaching as this values hijacking is, do not think for a moment that Satan is satisfied. On the contrary, he has his sights set on an even greater goal—to rule the world. Nothing short of sitting in Earth's pilot seat will do for him. But why?

THE DEVIL'S DREAM HAS A NAME

We do not know precisely when Satan fell and was decisively expelled from heaven, but some speculate it was sometime not long after day seven of creation (Genesis 3:2–3).[1] But regardless of the timing of his fall, Satan did not simply resign himself to defeat. He entertained no thoughts of riding into the sunset to lead an obscure existence. There was no remorse for his blasphemous offense, no repentance, and no regret. Instead, he continued swelling with arrogance. His unholy ambition became even more emboldened. Instead of surrendering, the devil simply regrouped, reloaded, and prepared himself for a long-term battle campaign against the King of kings. His next strategic strike against the Creator would be to go after creation itself, specifically the newly formed garden couple. Adam was God's prototype, the federal head of the human race. He and his wife, Eve, who were innocent of sin, became the bull's-eye target of the great deceiver. And what was Satan's original seductive message to humankind?

"You can be like God."

Wait, where have we heard that same idea before?

> But you said in your heart,
> "I will ascend to heaven;
> I will raise my throne above the stars of God,
> And I will sit on the mount of assembly
> In the recesses of the north.
> "I will ascend above the heights of the clouds;
> I will make myself like the Most High."
> (Isaiah 14:13–14)

As Jesus declared, "The evil man out of the evil treasure brings forth what is evil; for his mouth speaks from that which fills his heart" (Luke 6:45). When Satan tempts us to worship self, he is doing what comes naturally for him. He is acting out of the essence of who he is.

Thanks to his deliberate deception and Adam's willingness to trust someone other than his God, a path of pride and self-deceit can be traced throughout humanity's story. We see it in Noah's generation, so deeply enamored with self and sin that Moses recorded, "Then the LORD saw that the wickedness of man was great on the earth, and that every intent of the thoughts of his heart was only evil *continually*" (Genesis 6:5, emphasis added). We see it in Nimrod, the great-grandson of Noah. The name "Nimrod" in Hebrew means "rebel," and this "mighty hunter" and founder of the kingdom of Babel lived up to his name (Genesis 10–11). Whether he was directly involved with the design and building of the Tower of Babel is a matter of debate. But his prideful spirit certainly inspired the construction of such a structure that represented world rebellion against heaven.[2] Other pagan, pride-filled rulers would follow in their own quests for world domination—Pharaoh, Nebuchadnezzar, Alexander the Great, Caesar, conquerors, kings, and dictators, including Stalin and Hitler. If the truth were known, how many millions of people, if given the opportunity to rule the world like a god, would jump at the chance?

However, Satan is reserving that right for himself.

Both Scripture and history testify to the fact that the devil *still* wants to be in charge. And yet, thus far, he has been prevented from seeing his dream become reality. But the clock is ticking, the hour is late, and his day is coming, although not until heaven permits it. Satan does not determine the signs of the times or the times of the signs. God alone has sovereignly scripted the prophetic plan for the last days. And though Satan has his own end-times agenda, it will have to wait until the appointed time.

A chief tenet of that plan includes assuming the role of El Elyôn and ruling like the "God Most High, possessor of heaven and earth" (Genesis 14:19).[3] The Bible predicts that one day he will accomplish that dream through a *man*. And maybe sooner than we expect.

Through simultaneously mimicking and mocking heaven's sovereign reign, Satan will effectively forge God's signature on the title deed to planet Earth and humanity. He will do that through three unholy objectives: independence, authority, and worship.

The man, Antichrist, will be the vessel through whom Satan realizes his blasphemous and long-sought desires. It is by way of him that the devil channels his deepest, darkest cravings. Through the coming man of lawlessness, an ancient evil is unleashed upon the earth. During the Antichrist's rise to power, deception and destruction converge like raging rivers to form a mighty torrent of terror. Like the one who empowers him, the Antichrist's heart is baptized in sin, enflamed with self-love, and engorged with an insatiable desire to *be like God*. He is energized by evil, deputized by the devil, and saturated in "satanic pride" (Ezekiel 28:2, 9–12; Daniel 8:25; Revelation 13:4). And he is possessed—body, mind, and soul—by the Prince of Darkness.

And so, the rebellion that began in heaven long ago will one day culminate in the arrival of the one Scripture calls "the king (who) will do as he pleases" (Daniel 11:36).

Friend, a global darkness is coming to your world, and it has a name.

BECOMING ONE

American poet William Ross Wallace penned his most famous composition extolling the virtue and powerful influence of motherhood (yet another concept currently being redefined and suffering under attack). In his closing line, he stated, "For the hand that rocks the cradle / Is the hand that rules the world."[4]

While Wallace's poem certainly has merit and bears witness to the character and importance of motherhood, Bible prophecy has a slightly different take on who ascends to exercise power over the planet, particularly in the last days. According to Scripture, Satan has no plans to share his world rule with anyone, and especially not women (Daniel 11:37). But in order for the devil to accomplish this lofty goal through the Antichrist, he must first prepare a path toward global unity.

Unity.

That is another noble and wonderful virtue being hijacked today. But someone may object, "Wait, what's so bad about world unity? Isn't that a good thing? Why wouldn't we want the nations to come together? Wouldn't that help solve a lot of problems? Wouldn't this unity aid us in fighting common enemies—such as pandemics, diseases, pollution, hunger, the prospect of nuclear war, sex trafficking, or any other force that poses an existential threat to humankind? How could anyone be against *that*? Besides, doesn't the Bible also positively promote unity as a good thing? Why then would anyone be against global unity?"

Good questions.

To begin with, unity never exists in a valueless or meaningless context. It requires a common purpose. It necessitates a value around which it is built. The nobility of unity is determined by what it points to. So the real question is, "Precisely around *what* are we seeking to be unified?" What is the particular unity based on? What common belief, value, cause, or pursuit brings us together? What is the "glue" uniting us?

The terrorists who attacked the United States on September 11, 2001, were 100 percent unified in their objective. Hitler's Germany was a unified country during World War II. Angry Antifa mobs are unified in destroying businesses and seizing power over cities. So unity itself cannot be the ultimate goal.

For their part in the last days, Satan, his Antichrist, and the false prophet will manage to achieve a triunity never before seen, and one surpassed only by the unity of the real Trinity—Father, Son, and Holy Spirit. Scripture's prophecies state that the devil will indeed succeed in persuading world leaders to lay aside their national differences, merging into a new "oneness," or what Scripture refers to as a "common purpose" (Revelation 17:12, 17). But just how does he achieve his objective? What are the means to this evil end? And what does the Antichrist's global reset look like?

ONE-WORLD PEACE

Every year since 1945 the *Bulletin of the Atomic Scientists* has released its "Doomsday Clock" announcement, a metaphorical way of measuring how close scientists believe humanity is to experiencing an "existential catastrophe," one that threatens our very existence on planet Earth. In their 2021 assessment, as you recall from chapter 1, they declared us to be "100 seconds to midnight," the closest we have ever been to "the end" in their seventy-six-year history. Accurately dismissing the COVID-19 pandemic as not something that will "obliterate civilization," these scientists then turned to more threatening issues, like the potential for the world to "stumble into nuclear war."[5] Our current "dark nuclear landscape," they claim, has more potential at the moment to plunge us into global catastrophe than any other single factor. The United States (recently listed as the country posing the greatest threat to world peace) joins Russia, North Korea, and China as a top proliferator of these doomsday weapons of war.

WAR AND PEACE

Strangely absent in the scientists' assessment of global danger is Israel and the ongoing simmering tensions in the Middle East. In just over a week's time in May 2021, 4,369 rockets were fired into Israel from the Palestinian-occupied Gaza. Fortunately, over 90 percent were intercepted by Israel's "Iron Dome" missile defense system.[6] This is not a small thing, because military conflict between Israel and her close Arab neighbors could quickly boil over into other Muslim nations, creating a regional skirmish drawing in other countries like Russia, for example. Suffice it to say that whoever can bring peace to that region would be hailed as a darling diplomat and world leader.

Scripture claims this is precisely what is going to happen. In Daniel 9:27 the prophet described the event that will prove to be the "game changer" of the end times: "He will make a firm covenant with the many for one week, but in the middle of the week he will put a stop to sacrifice and grain offering; and on the wing of abominations will come one who makes desolate, even until a complete destruction, one that is decreed, is poured out on the one who makes desolate."

From the context of this passage, the "many" here refers to the people of Israel. So an individual, presumably an established or rising world leader, will broker a deal with the nation of Israel that is designed to last for one "week" (i.e., seven years).[7] This peace agreement will somehow facilitate the rebuilding of the Jewish (third) temple in Jerusalem (keep in mind, there has not been a Jewish temple in Jerusalem since AD 70, when it was destroyed by the Roman general Titus, exactly as Jesus prophesied in Matthew 24:1–2 and Luke 19:44). However, the significance of such a peace agreement will reverberate across the world. In fact, this treaty is officially what will restart God's prophetic clock once again.

Obviously, for the Jews to rebuild their temple, Israel must first be a nation again and be living back in the land, a prophecy often repeated in the Old Testament (Jeremiah 30:1–5; Ezekiel 34:11–24; 37; Zechariah 10:6–10). This prophecy was initially fulfilled on May 14, 1948, and is continuing in its fulfillment as Jews from around the world are returning to the ancient land of their forefathers. In fact, more Jews are living in Israel today than anywhere else in the world (6.7 million).[8]

However, though the Jews occupy Israel and control Jerusalem, the problem with rebuilding their temple is that major obstacles stand in the way. The Jerusalem Islamic Waqf was given oversight to the area in 1967, where the Dome of the Rock and the Al-Aqsa Mosque are located, on the very spot where the new temple would be built. So something or someone must remove those edifices before construction can begin. Obviously, those Muslim holy sites are not going away unless the forces of Islam are somehow no longer able to defend them. This leads many prophecy scholars to conclude that the Gog-Magog war will occur around the time of the Antichrist's covenant with Israel. Is it possible that his covenant somehow includes subverting Islamic forces? Could his agreement with Israel facilitate the razing of these structures to make way for the Jews to begin construction? Or his covenant with Israel may provide a protection plan, prompting the aforementioned Gog-Magog alliance (all Muslim nations with the exception of Russia) to attempt an invasion of Israel (Ezekiel 38–39). It is also possible that Israel may be invaded just prior to the Antichrist's peace treaty being signed. Perhaps he even spins it to somehow claim credit for Israel's victory—or at least capitalizes on it by offering Israel further protection as they begin building the temple. However, for the Gog-Magog invasion to take place, Israel must be "living securely" in the land (Ezekiel 38:8, 11, 14).[9] An established peace plan may be what brings that sense of security to them.[10]

PEACE AND SAFETY

Another component of the end times (and specifically the seven-year tribulation period) involves a tripart series of divine judgments on planet Earth and its citizens. What is worth noting is that every person acknowledges that these judgments are from "the Lamb," Jesus Christ (Revelation 6:15–17). These are called the seal, trumpet, and bowl judgments. However, earlier, John unveiled for us the first set of seal judgments the Lamb unleashes on humanity during the tribulation: "I looked, and behold, a white horse, and he who sat on it had a bow; and a crown was given to him, and he went out conquering and to conquer" (Revelation 6:2).

This Revelation prophecy seamlessly dovetails with Daniel's, not only in its nature but also its timing. Bible scholars carefully point out that this first of four apocalyptic riders carries a bow, yet no arrows are mentioned. This likely signifies that he will conquer or ascend to power not through bringing open warfare but rather through brokering peace. His establishment of peace is the initial means by which he establishes himself as a global force to be reckoned with. The immediate context of this passage also supports this view, as just two verses later, the second rider takes "peace from the earth" (Revelation 6:4). Clearly, in order for the second rider to take peace from the earth, peace must first have been established. And considering that a season of chaos and turmoil will follow the pretribulation rapture, the planet will be longing for calm and stability.

Paul echoed this spirit in 1 Thessalonians 5:2–3: "For you yourselves know full well that the day of the Lord will come just like a thief in the night. While they are saying, 'Peace and safety!' then destruction will come upon them suddenly like labor pains upon a woman with child, and they will not escape."

This peaceful rider will bring a message of hope. And in this instance, the Antichrist's pen will indeed be mightier than the sword. One can only imagine how the *Bulletin of the Atomic Scientists* will readjust its Doomsday Clock assessment when this historic treaty is signed.

ONE-WORLD GOVERNMENT

The peace achieved by the Antichrist partners with his rise to the pinnacle of the political world. Traditionally, when talk of a "one-world leader" arises, the majority of people reject the idea, and rightfully so. All past attempts and examples of world domination have ended badly.

No one would consciously desire an authoritarian despot to rule the world. However, as global crises become more acute and threaten peace and world health, it will become more acceptable for a single leader to step forward and unite the world's nations under a common flag. That is precisely what Scripture predicts is going to happen.

As we have said, it has long been Satan's ambition to rule the world. But to do this, he must first persuade countries to cast aside their nationalism and their differences and come together for the common good of all. This is the spirit behind the European Union and the WEF, who both have formed alliances with nations and global leaders to serve humanity and the planet. Whether the devil will utilize either of these entities as tools toward his ominous agenda remains to be seen. What is certain, however, is that in the last days a world empire will form, and the Antichrist will reign over it.

GAME OF THRONES

In Daniel 2 the prophet is called upon to interpret a dream of King Nebuchadnezzar. This dream had to do with the future of the world and the key nations in power. In his vision, Nebuchadnezzar saw a statue with a head of gold, chest and arms of silver, middle and thighs of bronze, legs of iron, and feet partly of iron and partly of clay. Daniel confidently declared to the king that although his administration's enchanters, magicians, and astrologers were unable to interpret his dream, there "is a God in heaven who reveals mysteries, and He has made known to King Nebuchadnezzar what will take place in the latter days" (Daniel 2:28).

Daniel then interpreted the dream, explaining to the king that Nebuchadnezzar was the head of gold and that the rest of the statue's parts represented three successive kingdoms that would arise after him. The fourth of these kingdoms would be as strong as iron, crushing all others (Daniel 2:40). This empire would be both strong and brittle, represented by the ten toes of the statue, which were composed partly of clay and partly of iron. He finished the interpretation by telling of a final kingdom that would be established by God and would put an end to all these man-made kingdoms (Daniel 2:44–45). Daniel concluded by announcing that "the great God has made known to the king what will take place in the future; so the dream is true and its interpretation is trustworthy" (Daniel 2:45).

Jumping forward about fifty years, Daniel had his own vision. In it he saw "four great beasts" coming out of the sea: a lion with eagle's wings, a lopsided bear with three ribs in its mouth, a leopard with four wings of a bird on its back (and also four heads), and a fourth beast described as "dreadful and ter-rifying and extremely strong" (Daniel 7:3–7). Its strength was pictured in its iron teeth, which devoured other nations. This beast also had ten horns, augmented by "another horn, a little one" (Daniel 7:8). Daniel's own explanation, as well as a survey of history, enables us to easily identify the symbolism represented in both the statue and the four beasts (Daniel 7:15–17).

Head of gold / winged lion = Babylon
Chest and arms of silver / lopsided bear = Medo-Persia
Middle and thighs of bronze / four-winged leopard =
    Greece
Legs of iron, feet of iron and clay / ten-horned beast =
    Rome

The two legs of the statue represent the fact that the Roman Empire was eventually split into East (Constantinople) and West (Rome) in the third century. This part is plain and easy to interpret. However, two curious pieces of this prophetic puzzle remain conspicuously absent from a survey of history, particularly regarding the last kingdom—Rome.

First, in Nebuchadnezzar's vision, a "stone" struck the statue and became "a great mountain and filled the whole earth" (Daniel 2:35). This would seem to indicate that Rome was conquered by a more powerful kingdom, but history records nothing resembling this. In reality, the Roman Empire declined slowly, with the western empire eventually collapsing in AD 476 and the eastern empire gradually deteriorating and falling in the fifteenth century. No one empire suddenly ended Rome's dominance, and no stone kingdom has ever appeared.

The second puzzling prophecy depicts Rome and the imagery of the ten toes and ten horns. Daniel explains these to be ten kings (see also Revelation 13:1; 17:12). But again, Rome never existed in a ten-king federation, or anything close to it. Therefore, both of these prophecies must await a future fulfillment. We can conclude that in the latter days, the fourth kingdom (Rome) will arise once again in a "new expression," or form, this time consisting of ten kings, or nations (Daniel 7:24). In addition to these ten kings, an eleventh king (a little horn) will arise and put down three of the existing kings, replacing them. This little horn will rule over the ten-nation alliance for "time, times, and half a time," or forty-two months (Daniel 7:25). This also matches the time frame given by John concerning the final three and a half years of the Antichrist's reign during the tribulation (Revelation 12:14; 13:5).

Therefore, the Bible prophesies that in the last days, a "Revived Roman Empire" will rise, led by a man referred to as the Antichrist (or the Beast). But it bears repeating: Why would anyone, liberal or conservative, be in favor of such a united kingdom and ruler? It has to do with who he is, when he appears, and how he presents himself. This man will not come to power dressed as a dictator but rather as a savior. He will be a consummate diplomat (Daniel 8:23–25). A man of peace (Daniel 9:27; Revelation 6:1–2). A "prince" with a persona that exudes charisma and charm (Daniel 7:8, 11; 8:23). We have watched in recent history as relatively obscure political figures have emerged seemingly out of nowhere to assume powerful positions. Most notably in America, Barack Obama, Donald Trump, and Kamala Harris. However, none of these were preceded by the kind of global crisis necessary to welcome one man to lead the entire planet toward a global reset of peace and prosperity.

But such a man is on his way and may very well be alive today.

FOUR

666 AND THE COMING CASHLESS SOCIETY

"It's the economy, stupid" is a phrase coined by James Carville, a strategist for the successful presidential campaign of Bill Clinton in 1992. The popular slogan expresses the universal truism that most issues can be boiled down to basic economics. Carville's slogan has not been lost on the great resetters. While the strategies of the global reset are coordinated and complex, the aim of it all is simple yet sinister: Control. Total control. Global control. Iron-fisted control. Global authoritarianism is their intended goal. But harnessing total sway over the planet requires more than governmental and political control. To put their plan into place, the global resetters must seize control over the economy as well. They realize all too well, "It's the economy, stupid."

The great reset, while popularized in recent days, is not new. It began in earnest with the financial meltdown in the late 2000s.

When the WEF gathered in January 2009, the two thousand business and political leaders described the world economic disaster as a "crisis of confidence." The official theme of the 2009 forum was "Shaping the Post-Crisis World."[1] Klaus Schwab, the brainchild of the great reset, referred to the global economic meltdown as a "transformational crisis." He urged the delegates to respond to the crisis by shaping a "new world" order. Schwab said, "Above all else this is a crisis of confidence. To restore confidence you have to establish signposts that the world after the crisis will be different. We have to create a new world."[2] He also announced the launch of a "Global Redesign Initiative" to rebuild the global economic system.[3]

The financial crisis of the late 2000s has faded in the rearview mirror, yet much of what we see today is driven by a feeling that the financial crisis of the late 2000s was a massive missed opportunity. The global resetters were not fully able to capitalize on their stated goals in the wake of the financial meltdown. The open window of opportunity slowly closed, but with the rise of COVID-19, they found the perfect catalyst to reboot and accelerate their stated goal of a new world order. The global resetters are committed to not repeating their mistake. They are zealously seizing the moment and momentum of the COVID-19 crisis to remake society on every front, especially the economy. The chaos that began in 2020 and continues is not an accident. As Elijah Mvundura notes, "The full economic, political, and social meaning and significance of the COVID-19 [pandemic] has yet to reveal itself. It is clear, however, that it has accelerated trends that were already eroding the foundations of freedom, order, and reason."[4] For instance, COVID-19 is fast-tracking widespread economic dependence on the government. Erwin Lutzer notes:

> Government assurances are designed to create a dependency on the state.... Here in America, a boost to such dependency took place when trillions of dollars were created electronically for the massive government bailouts in the wake of the COVID-19 pandemic. Going forward, we can expect calls for more government intervention, more government control, and increased redistribution of resources....
>
> ... Healthcare, guaranteed wage and price controls, free college tuition, and assured comfortable retirement are all part of its larger agenda.[5]

COVID-19 is the crisis de jure that justifies all kinds of economic control. Climate change is the next global crisis waiting in the wings. It is already being leveraged to build on the control agenda and take it much further than the pandemic. Inflation may be the next crisis that can be exploited. Crises, whether real or imagined, are being weaponized by global elites to justify giant power grabs and impose greater controls on an increasingly passive populace.

Crisis politics keeps everyone on edge. It sows seeds of fear and panic. Over time it creates an environment where people are willing to do anything or surrender any right to solve the "crisis." Issues like the pandemic, climate change, and inflation are not so much calamities to be solved but crises to be exploited. Whatever the crisis, the solution is always the same—bigger government. The authoritarian impulse is accelerating on every front. The tentacles of authoritarianism reach far and wide. The groundwork is being laid to create submissive citizens who are dependent and conditioned to bow the knee to edicts handed down from on high.

QUICK CASH

While there will no doubt be many twists and turns in the march to global economic domination, the quickest, simplest way to take the reins of the world economy is to implement a global cashless economy—a cashless revolution. "'The great reset' has been used nearly interchangeably with 'the global currency reset.'"[6] The world is entering "a so-called Fourth Industrial (Digital) Revolution."[7]

Daily headlines are announcing its imminent arrival:

"The Birth of the Cashless Society," the Corbett Report, August 30, 2020

"Our Cash-Free Future Is Getting Closer," *New York Times*, July 6, 2020

"U.S. Moves Closer to Digital Dollar," *Forbes*, July 1, 2020

"Bank of England Governor Signals Central Bank Digital Currency Is Coming," Steven Guinness, July 15, 2020

"China Creates Its Own Digital Currency, a First for Major Economy," *Wall Street Journal*, April 5, 2021

"China's Rising Cashless Society," Eye on Asia, October 2020

"Reports Indicate That Sweden Will Stop Using Cash by 2023," Futurism, October 10, 2017

Economic experts say we are rocketing toward a cashless society. The majority of people now use noncash payments by choice, but in the very near future there may be no choice. The long-term shift from cash has been ongoing for some time, but COVID-19 has dramatically accelerated the trend that was already underway. During the pandemic, most stores and restaurants that remained open would only accept credit or debit payments. Contaminated cash was not accepted. In the aftermath of the pandemic, the cashless trajectory is rising.

China, where the world's first recognizable coins were produced more than three thousand years ago, is leading the transition to the cashless system. If you visit China today, "there's a strong chance you'll see people paying for things using facial recognition on their phones."[8] "In the aftermath of the COVID-19 pandemic, China has launched its digital currency, the digital yuan or renminbi (RMB), in its bid to become a cashless society using contactless payments and is poised to become the first country in the world to do so."[9] Digitalized money is a resetter's dream, allowing them to track global spending in real time.

For China, the move to digital currency is a further expansion of its sweeping surveillance society that controls its citizens.

China's version of a digital currency is controlled by its central bank, which will issue the new electronic money. It is expected to give China's government vast new tools to monitor both its economy and its people. The digital yuan has not replaced the paper currency but is functioning alongside it. It's also trackable, adding another tool to China's heavy state surveillance.[10]

To keep up with China, digitizing the dollar is a very high priority on the fed's agenda in the United States.

All these developments are paving the way for the resetter's agenda. The title "The Great Reset" is being employed by globalists "as a smokescreen to smuggle through one of their most cherished fantasies: the cashless society. Soon, central banks will be issuing national digital currencies and tracking every single transaction in the economy in real time."[11]

The practical, expedient advantages of going cashless are often touted:

- It eliminates the expense of producing, storing, and securing paper money.
- It crushes counterfeiting of currency.
- It reduces tax evasion and money laundering.
- It diminishes the spread of disease (during the coronavirus outbreak, most stores that were open stopped accepting cash to decrease the spread of the virus).
- It hamstrings organized crime and illegal drug trade that is fueled by cash transactions.

Yet, as attractive as these justifications are, do not be fooled. There is one main impetus behind the move toward cashless. Cashless equals control. When cashless is king, every economic transaction will be documented. The powers that be will know who is spending, what they are spending, and how they are spending. That is the goal. The cashless society is about so much more than just how we pay for things at the store or online. It is intricately tethered to a system of persistent technological surveillance that represents the ultimate control over our lives. In an article on the WEF website, the author acknowledges the move toward greater government control. "This is my vision of a true cashless society. There is an exchange of value in its entirety—just like cash. And it requires a national government—rather than banks or the like—to act as the payment provider, effectively becoming a state-backed utility."[12]

The goal is for national governments, and ultimately a global government, to control the cashless currency. Eventually, it will all be in the hands of a global government, which will thereby control everything. The WEF article continues:

> If everyone were connected to an end-to-end e-payment infrastructure—a cashless environment—there would be transparency in money flows. Whether it's international aid or private investment, if everyone in the chain were connected digitally, you could see where the money went and how it was spent.
>
> Any sums appearing outside of that framework could immediately be flagged and investigated. This would narrow the focus for law enforcement and forensic accountants, making it easier to target and recoup hidden money.[13]

That may sound good to the resetters, but it should set off alarm bells for lovers of freedom and personal autonomy. Just as big media is controlling and suppressing the flow of information it deems objectionable, the overlords of the cashless system will control the flow of finances. They will know where every dollar originates and where it is spent. Cashless will allow all financial transactions to be tracked and traced. Any transactions they do not approve will quickly be disallowed and terminated. Big

Brother will control everything that is bought and sold. Looking ahead, David Solway warns:

> Society will become "cashless" and all standard monetary transactions replaced by digital currency and governed by electronic means, which can be cancelled by reigning authority at the slightest provocation. Debts will be forgiven and creditors will face the prospect of bankruptcy. The middle class and small entrepreneurs will be wiped out. Commerce will become progressively "contact-less."[14]

CRYPTO-CASHLESS

Another important development on the cashless front is the stunning emergence of cryptocurrencies. Bitcoin, the initial cryptocurrency, launched in 2009. As of January 2021, four thousand cryptocurrencies—and counting—existed. The transformative year for cryptocurrencies was 2019, but in the succeeding years their expansion shows no signs of slowing. While undergoing erratic fluctuations, Bitcoin has climbed to astronomical valuation. In the United Kingdom, cryptocurrencies can be used to purchase automobiles. Tesla announced its acceptance of Bitcoin for payment in 2021, which caused the value to soar, but Elon Musk quickly reversed the position over climate concerns. One National Football League (NFL) player elected to take his salary in Bitcoin.[15] Cryptocurrencies show every sign of advancing and accelerating for the foreseeable future.

One of the major appeals of cryptocurrencies, other than

the prospect that they will steadily increase in value, is that they decentralize control over currency. On the other hand, digital currency issued by central banks is an attempt to centralize and exert greater economic control and stability. So, as you can imagine, there is an inevitable clash brewing between digital currencies issued by central banks and cryptocurrencies. Time will tell how it all shakes out. Nevertheless, one thing is clear: digital and cryptocurrencies foreshadow a digitized future for money and a cashless economic system. Together, they are another mile marker on the road to cashless control.

MARK IT DOWN

From earlier chapters about the rise of the Antichrist, we know where this is all headed. The great reset and its cashless agenda are a catalyst and necessary antecedent for the one-world economy of the Antichrist. Ancient prophecies in Scripture lay out the scenario in full color. History is headed toward a one-world government under the total control of Satan's superman, the final Antichrist who will subjugate the planet. To bring his control to fruition, this final ruler will have to control global commerce and impose a one-world economy. Without economic control, there is no real control. The control of the Antichrist over the world economy will undoubtedly precede and promote his rise to global political power.

Revelation 6:5–6 describes a global financial crisis during the final time of tribulation, resulting from hyperinflation that results in crippling famine. "When He opened the third seal, I heard the third living creature say, 'Come and see.' So I looked, and behold, a black horse, and he who sat on it had a pair of scales in his hand. And I heard a voice in the midst of the four living creatures saying, 'A quart of wheat for a denarius, and three quarts of barley for a denarius; and do not harm the oil and the wine'" (NKJV).

The inflation will be so severe that it will take everything a person can earn in one day just to put food on the table. This runaway financial crisis will certainly be seized upon by the Antichrist, who will leverage the global instability to gain a stronger foothold and inaugurate a one-world economic system. The global spending spree in the United States and other nations in the wake of COVID-19 is already fueling inflation and could be a precursor to what lies ahead when the tribulation period erupts.

The biblical starting point for the one-world, end-time economic system is Revelation 13:16–18:

> And he causes all, the small and the great, and the rich and the poor, and the free men and the slaves, to be given a mark on their right hand or on their forehead, and he provides that no one will be able to buy or to sell, except the one who has the mark, either the name of the beast or the number of his name. Here is wisdom. Let him who has understanding calculate the number of the beast, for the number is that of a man; and his number is six hundred and sixty-six [666].

The Bible clearly links the universal mark of the Beast system with the emergence of a cashless society, where all commerce is centralized and controlled by one entity. If all transactions are cashless, the government or ruling commercial authorities will know where every dollar comes from and where every dollar goes. Nothing will escape their notice. They will be able to control every financial transaction. Those who fail to comply with their directives will be locked out of the economy. That is total economic control, and that is the scope of influence prophesied in Revelation 13:16–18.

THE MEANING OF THE MARK

The mark of the Beast has been related to all kinds of modern technology. But it seems to be nothing more complicated than a visible tattoo or etching on the right hand or forehead. Henry Morris provided an excellent description of the nature of the mark:

> The word itself ("mark") is the Greek *charagma*. It is used only in Revelation, to refer to the mark of the beast (eight times), plus one time to refer to idols "*graven* by art and man's device" (Acts 17:29). The mark is something like an etching or a tattoo which, once inscribed, cannot be removed, providing a permanent (possibly eternal) identification as a follower of the beast and the dragon.[16]

When it comes to the exact nature of the mark of the Beast, the answer is, we really do not know, and we should not waste a lot of time thinking about it.

THE SIGNIFICANCE OF 666

As you can imagine, there is endless speculation about the meaning of 666. The best view, however, is that Revelation 13:16–18 refers to what is known as *gematria*, that is, attributing a numerical value to each of the letters of the alphabet. Hebrew, Latin, Greek, and English all have numerical values for each letter in the alphabet. For the Hebrew language, each letter in the twenty-two-letter Hebrew alphabet is assigned a numerical value as follows: 1, 2, 3, 4, 5, 6, 7, 8, 9, 10, 20, 30, 40, 50, 60, 70, 80, 90, 100, 200, 300, and 400. Employing gematria, a numerical value can be assigned to any word or name by adding together the numerical value of each of its letters. In Revelation 13, a numerical value for the Antichrist's name is intended since the one with wisdom is to "calculate" or "count" the number. To count the number of a name means simply to add up the numbers attached to all the letters in the name.

Revelation 13:16–18 lays out five key pointers that inform our interpretation of the mark of the Beast and support the idea that gematria is intended. Note the sequence:

1. The name of the Beast
2. The number representing his name
3. The number of the Beast
4. The number of a man
5. The number is 666[17]

Tracking these five phrases in a logical progression, the number or mark of the Beast is the number of a man, and further, it is the precise numerical value of the Antichrist's name. Prophecy scholar Arnold Fruchtenbaum supports this view:

> In this passage whatever the personal name of the Antichrist will be, if his name is spelled out in Hebrew characters, the numerical value of his name will be 666. So this is the number that will be put on the worshipers of the Antichrist. Since a number of different calculations can equal 666, it is impossible to figure the name out in advance. But when he does appear, whatever his personal name will be, it will equal 666. Those who are wise (verse 18) at that time will be able to point him out.[18]

When the Antichrist emerges on the world scene at the commencement of the tribulation, those who know God's Word will be able to identify him by the number of his name—666.

Over the years, many have engaged in reckless speculation and misused gematria by applying it to the names of modern leaders to try to identify the Antichrist. All such foolish speculation should be shunned and denounced because according to Scripture, the Antichrist will not be unveiled until after the rapture of believers to heaven. He will be disclosed at the beginning of the tribulation period or "day of the Lord" (2 Thessalonians 2:2–3). At that time, believers on earth, who have come to Christ after the rapture, will be able to identify him because the number of his name will be 666. "Here is wisdom. Let him who has understanding calculate the number of the beast, for the number is that of a man; and his number is six hundred and sixty-six" (Revelation 13:18).

Let me assure you, you do not want to know the identity of the Antichrist. Since the rapture will occur before the Antichrist rises, if you ever do figure out who the Antichrist is, I have bad news for you—you have been left behind!

Many prophecy teachers have pointed out that six is the number of humanity in Scripture (the man and woman were created on the sixth day). Thus, the triple six highlights man's attempt to take the place of God, yet falling short of God's perfect number, seven. Prophecy scholar John Walvoord wrote:

In the Book of Revelation, the number "7" is one of the most significant numbers indicating perfection. . . . This beast claims to be God, and if that were the case, he should be 777. This passage, in effect, says, No, you are only 666. You are short of deity even though you were originally created in the image and likeness of God.[19]

Bible teacher M. R. De Haan also held this view.

Six is the number of man. Three is the number of divinity. Here is the interpretation. The Beast will be a man who claims to be God. Three sixes imply that he is a false god and a deceiver, but he is nevertheless merely a man, regardless of his claims. Seven is the number of divine perfection, and 666 is one numeral short of seven. This man of sin will reach the highest peak of power and wisdom, but he will still be merely man.[20]

In his sovereignty, and to spotlight the symbolism, God will see to it that the numerical value of the Antichrist's name equals the number of humanity—three times over.

THE PURPOSE OF THE MARK

During the coming time of tribulation, the mark of the Beast will serve two primary functions. First, it will serve as a visible sign of loyalty, devotion, and allegiance to the Antichrist. Think about it. The Antichrist's mark, the numerical value of his name, will be etched or imprinted on the right hand or forehead of those who surrender to his will. He will literally put his name on them. He will own them. Everywhere they go, the first thing people will see is the number of the Antichrist emblazoned on their forehead or right hand. Taking the mark of the Beast will not be an inadvertent, unintended act. Taking the mark will involve a conscious choice to accept the Antichrist as God.

Second, the mark will be the global passport to participate in the economy. During the final half of the tribulation, this literal, visible mark will be mandatory for any commercial transaction (Revelation 13:17). No one outside this system will be able to engage in any business or commerce. Some of the proposals in the wake of the pandemic preview this kind of control. In many major US cities, a vaccination card must be shown to enter gyms and restaurants. There has been growing momentum of COVID-19 vaccination passports being required to travel. "Denmark, the U.K., China, Singapore, Malaysia, and India have also developed vaccine passports."[21]

The European Union has launched a digital pass system to let residents prove they have been vaccinated against COVID-19, recovered from the disease, or recently tested negative for the virus, allowing them to travel freely among all twenty-seven member nations.

For months Israelis used a similar digital pass system,

showing their vaccination status to enter restaurants, gyms, and other venues. And Australia and Japan have rolled out digital proof of vaccination certificates too.[22]

These kinds of digital validation measures faintly foreshadow what is coming in the end times.

The spiritual implications of the mark of the Beast are sobering. When the Beast, or Antichrist, seizes the levers of global power at the middle of the tribulation, every person on earth will be faced with an epic choice. Swear allegiance to the man who claims to be God, giving up ownership of one's life to him, or bow the knee to the true God and forfeit one's right to buy and sell and even face beheading (Revelation 20:4).

The Antichrist's economic agenda will be straightforward: take my name on you and worship me, or starve. Every person on earth, left behind after the rapture, will face the ultimate spiritual decision, and the consequence of that decision could not be more serious. All the mark takers will face the eternal, unmitigated wrath of God.

Then another angel, a third one, followed them, saying with a loud voice, "If anyone worships the beast and his image, and receives a mark on his forehead or on his hand, he also will drink of the wine of the wrath of God, which is mixed in full strength in the cup of His anger; and he will be tormented with fire and brimstone in the presence of the holy angels and in the presence of the Lamb. And the smoke of their torment goes up forever and ever; they have no rest day and night, those who worship the beast and his image, and whoever receives the mark of his name." (Revelation 14:9–11)

Taking the mark will ultimately be a spiritual decision; the economic ramifications will be secondary to this fateful decision every person on earth will face.

Ten Keys to Understanding the Mark of the Beast

» The mark is future, not past or present.

» The mark is a literal, visible brand, mark, or tattoo.

» It will be placed "upon" the right hand or forehead of people during the tribulation.

» The mark will be given as a sign of devotion to the Antichrist and as a passport to engage in commerce.

» The mark will be the number 666, which will be the numerical value of the Antichrist's name.

» Believers during the tribulation will be able to calculate the number and identify the Antichrist.

» Those who take the mark will be eternally doomed.

» Before the rapture, no one should attempt to identify the Antichrist or his mark—the number 666.

» While current technology and methods of identifying and locating people strikingly foreshadow the Antichrist's ability to control the world, no specific modern technology should be identified as the mark of the Beast. No one can say specifically what technology will be employed to fulfill this prophecy, but what we see today certainly makes such a system not only possible but probable.

» In spite of its association with evil, 666 will be received by those who willfully reject Christ during the tribulation.[23]

COVID-19 VACCINATION: THE MARK OF THE BEAST?

With the creation and mass distribution of vaccines for COVID-19, the question of whether these vaccines could be the mark of the Beast in Revelation 13 has been raised over and over. Many have expressed concerns that the vaccine may contain some kind of tracking device and that world governments may force people to take it to travel and engage in commerce, making it parallel to the mark. While believers may have personal or medical reasons for not taking a vaccine, fear that it may be the mark of the Beast is not a legitimate concern.

There are three main reasons COVID-19 vaccines cannot be the mark of the Beast. First, according to Revelation 13, the mark of the Beast will not be required and enforced until the Antichrist assumes global power at the midpoint of the final seven years of tribulation. We are not yet in the final time of tribulation predicted in Scripture. The rapture of the church has not occurred. The church of Jesus Christ is still on earth. The tribulation period, or "day of the Lord," has not arrived. Therefore, nothing we see today is the mark of the Beast. Pinpointing any current technology, vaccine, or method of identification as the mark of the Beast is jumping the gun.

Second, as we have already seen, the mark of the Beast is the numerical value of the final Antichrist's name, not a vaccine. Also, the mark is "upon" the right hand or the forehead, not injected into the upper arm.

Third, those who take the mark during the final years of the tribulation will be doomed for choosing the Antichrist over Jesus Christ and taking the Antichrist's mark upon them (Revelation 14:9–11). This means they take it willfully, voluntarily, and knowingly. No one will take the mark accidentally, casually, or by mistake. God will not doom people to an eternity separated from him for something they do mistakenly or innocently. During the tribulation, those on the earth will face a monumental, clear decision—take the Antichrist as God and receive his mark, or reject him and worship Jesus Christ alone as God and face the consequence of being locked out of the world economy and possibly martyred. Nothing even close to this is involved in taking a vaccine.

For these reasons, no believer should entertain any fear that the COVID-19 vaccine or any other current technology is the mark of the Beast. Having said that, the dictatorial control behind the mandate directives is paving the way for global compliance to take a government-required action in order to fully participate in the rights and privileges of citizenship. Satan is seizing every opportunity to prepare the world for his man and his plan.

GOD CONTROL

What is unfolding before our eyes on the economic front could be the genesis, the first dominoes to fall in a dramatic, tectonic shift to a global, digital economic system. A system that will ultimately be controlled by one man. A system that will ultimately require all people to be registered and submit to him—the final world order foretold by the biblical prophets long ago.

As fascinating and relevant as the cashless society and government control of the world economy are, there is one point we dare not miss. God's Word predicted almost two thousand years ago that just such a global system will rise in the end times. This is even more compelling when we remember that the words of Revelation 13 were penned by the apostle John in the age of wood, stones, swords, spears, and Roman togas. That long ago, who but the true and living God could have predicted a one-world economic system that controls global commerce? The prophecies in Revelation 13 and the developments we see today that strikingly foreshadow them are additional evidence that the God of the Bible is the only true and living God and that the Bible is his inspired, inerrant Word. The precision of the Bible's prophecies also demonstrates that God is the Sovereign over history who knows the future and brings his will to pass. These prophecies serve as undeniable proof that God is in control.

This should bring supreme comfort to everyone who reads these words. What we are seeing played out before our eyes is part of the divine script leading to the coming of Jesus Christ to take over planet Earth and bring it under his just, righteous, and benevolent rule. And the same God who rules time and nations rules the intimate details of your life and mine. God is sovereign. That is more than a sloppy, feel-good slogan. It is an immutable foundation we can build our lives upon as we await the coming of Christ.

FIVE

ENTER THE DRAGON: CHINA, THE RESET, AND THE END OF DAYS

From the 20th to the 24th of January, 2020, the 50th World Economic Forum [WEF] met in the Swiss city of Davos. At the same time, on January 23rd, China imposed the first lockdown in the history of humankind, and the global avalanche of corona coverage began. Just a few days later, [World Health Organization] WHO Director Tedros Adhanom Ghebreyesus was already praising China's method as "precedent-setting." Almost every country on earth copied China in the following months. In the meantime, Klaus Schwab, executive chairman of the WEF, was looking forward to the once-in-a-lifetime opportunity for a "Great Reset" that he conjured out of his hat in front of the global public in Davos. Each additional day of lockdown brings Big Tech, Big Pharma, and Big Money unbelievable profits. . . .

Wuhan was the first metropolis in the world to be locked down; 19 million people were locked up in their apartments for five weeks in its wake.[1]

One of the colossal changes of the twenty-first century is the political, economic, and military awakening of Asia—primarily China. The twenty-first century has been dubbed "the Chinese century."[2]

China, along with the great nations of Asia, situated east of the Euphrates River, slumbered for centuries but is beginning to stir and play a dominant role in international, socioeconomic, and political dynamics. With a population of 1.4 billion, the enormity of China's geography and population alone makes its development especially noteworthy. The People's Republic of China, ruled by the Chinese Communist Party (CCP), is flexing its muscles and expanding its influence around the globe at a rapidly accelerating pace.

China's development is being compared to the explosive growth in late nineteenth-century America, except that it is happening on a swifter and broader scale. Here are some eye-opening statistics about China today:

- China will overtake the United States to become the world's biggest economy in 2028, according to the Centre for Economics and Business Research. China's economic engine is running at full speed.
- China will take the top spot five years earlier than previously estimated, largely due to COVID-19 and the country's response.[3]
- China still regards Taiwan as a renegade province. Many

expect China to test US resolve with more aggression toward Taiwan.

- China's role in space is expanding dramatically. They want to dominate space in the next twenty years.[4]
- As of February 2021, about 1.6 billion mobile phone subscriptions had been registered in China.[5]

Understanding China's explosive, expanding role in the world today, even if there were no scripture suggesting its place in end-time events, it would only be natural to expect China to be part of the worldwide landscape in the end times.

GROUND ZERO

The meteoric rise of China is significant on many fronts, but one pivot point in China's rise is its emergence as a centerpiece in the great reset. In many ways, China is ground zero for the great reset. The current phase of the great reset started there: the pandemic. The spread. The lockdown. It all started there, and it all emanated and progressed from there. Yet, throughout the COVID-19 disaster, the great resetters have exonerated China, applauded China, and pointed to China as the kind of society the world needs to emulate. Klaus Schwab, the brainchild of the great reset, has aptly been called a "China fanboy."[6] He is also personally linked to China. His son Olivier Schwab, who has led the WEF office in Beijing since 2011, is married to a Chinese woman. Olivier has extolled China and stated that the West could learn as much from China as China could from the West.

During the COVID-19 pandemic, the WHO, which appears

to be an arm of the Communist Chinese government, has been an apologist and defender of China and has exerted unparalleled global authority. As Aya Velázquez said, "The WHO is acting as a kind of shadow world government and instrument for the lockdown-reset apologists by implementing agreed-upon measures through the health departments of individual countries."[7] The control being exerted by WHO and other health officials is a striking precursor to the kind of control global resetters desire for all people in all places. China is the template.

SURVEILLANCE SOCIETY

With a staggering population of 1.4 billion, China is the most authoritarian repressive nation in the world. China controls its massive population by threats and intimidation. The brutal response to the protests in Hong Kong shocked the world. One tool the CCP uses to control its populace is a draconian social credit system that ranks its citizens based on their "social credit." This system has been in the planning stages since 2009 but was officially rolled out in 2020, just in time for the plague. Most people are familiar with the idea of a credit score based on income level, so this may not strike us as too concerning at first blush. China's new social credit system, however, is something immeasurably different—and much darker. The basic underlying goal is whitewashing and blacklisting. "Through continuous digital surveillance, individuals are evaluated based upon every aspect of their behavior—and then issued a social reputation score."[8]

The social credit system is employed for individuals, corporations, companies, and even government agencies. Here is how it works: the government deploys hundreds of millions of facial-recognition cameras to monitor its population, sometimes using them to levy fines for activities such as jaywalking.

> Like private credit scores, a person's social score can move up and down depending on their behavior. . . . Examples of infractions include bad driving, smoking in non-smoking zones, buying too many video games, and posting fake news online, specifically about terrorist attacks or airport security.[9]

The punishments and penalties are meted out in various forms, such as travel bans, slow internet speeds, and exclusion from higher education. China has already started punishing people by restricting their travel, including banning them from flights.[10] In some cases, access to basic necessities can be limited or at least delayed, such as having to wait longer for health-care needs. Failing to fall in line with state-mandated social behaviors can result in denial of the ability to get a loan or purchase property. Companies and businesses are also scored. Those who fail to turn over vast quantities of customer data to the CCP are in danger of being fined or shut down by the government.

To speed up enforcement, a digital currency, which is in the works in China, would make it possible to both mete out and collect fines as soon as an infraction is detected.[11] Under this system, the Chinese populace is under the threatening thumb of the Communist Party in every area of life. "The system has been likened to science fiction scenarios depicting dystopian societies. . . . Many have compared it to some level of dystopian governance, such as in George Orwell's *1984* in which the state heavily controls every aspect of a citizen's life."[12]

In recent times, this has begun to hit a bit closer to home. During the recent lockdowns in the United States, restaurants and other places of business were threatened with fines or shutdowns if they ignored or failed to enforce various state and municipal mandates. Fear, propaganda, "science," public shaming, and government mandates were employed to secure submission. While not nearly as invasive or all-encompassing as the CCP social credit system, "the heavy-handed pandemic response by world leaders is preparing the world for the implementation of social credit systems to be rolled out in various forms and fashions around the world."[13] A global coup is clearly underway to wrest freedom and control from individuals and into the hands of governments and global elites in an attempt to enslave humanity under the rule of one man who is controlled by Satan.

CHINA LEADS THE WAY

Two main indicators point to China as an embryonic force in the global coup and conspiracy to distill power into the hands of a few. First, China was the source of the coronavirus that engulfed the globe in a matter of weeks, killing millions. China was also the first nation to lock down. That much is certain. What is not certain is where and how the virus was unleashed. At the time of writing, the precise genesis of the virus is still being hotly debated. Did it occur naturally in Wuhan wet markets and jump from animals to humans, or was it let loose accidentally in a lab leak, or even intentionally from the Wuhan Institute of Virology? China's stubborn stonewalling and resistance to any meaningful investigation may preclude any definitive conclusion. However, the question remains: If the virus arose naturally, what does China have to hide? Nevertheless, significant signs point toward the Wuhan Institute of Virology as the source of COVID-19. The fact that the virus erupted within a few blocks of the lab is a smoking gun. In any event, one thing is sure: China is the confirmed source of the COVID-19 pandemic that has provided the great resetters with the perfect storm to execute their plan for global transformation. And, so far, China has escaped any meaningful consequences.

Second, not only is China the source of the pandemic that changed the world, but the great resetters view China as the model for the authoritarian control they envision for the entire world. Klaus Schwab and others related to the WEF have applauded China's handling of the pandemic and hold China as the kind of society they want the world to emulate. As part of the plan, China is playing an increasing role in the WEF in recent years. Chinese functionaries have been attending the WEF since 2009. In recent years, hundreds of Chinese entrepreneurs can be found hustling about the forum.

The following quote is a bit lengthy but worth reading carefully because it provides an excellent analysis of China's relationship to the great reset.

China is the model for the economic and political system being promoted in the West . . .

The Great Reset represents the development of the Chinese system in the West, only in reverse. Whereas the Chinese political elite began with a socialist-communist political system and implemented "capitalism" later, the elite in the West began with "capitalism" and is aiming to implement a socialist-communist political system now. It's as if the Western oligarchy looked to the "socialism" on display in China, and said, "yes, we want it."

This explains many otherwise seeming contradictions, not the least of which is the leftist authoritarianism of Big Tech. Big Tech, and in particular Big Digital.[14]

The article continues:

The Chinese characteristics that the Great Reset aims to reproduce in connection with Western capitalism would resemble the totalitarianism of the CCP. It would require a great abridgement of individual rights—including property rights, free expression, freedom of movement, freedom of association, freedom of religion, and the free enterprise system as we understand it.

The Great Reset would implement the political system in much the same way as China has done—with 5G-enabled smart city surveillance, the equivalent of social credit scores, medical passports, political imprisonment, and other means of social and political repression and control.[15]

The final result of this movement will be socialism and capitalism with Chinese characteristics that, in essence, are the same thing.[16]

If the global resetters succeed, this system will go global. Every person who can be sufficiently surveilled will be part of a global social credit network through which desired behaviors (such as getting the COVID-19 vaccine) could be enforced, and undesired behaviors could be eliminated or at least drastically reduced.

China's role in the great reset is becoming clearer as each day passes, but does this carry any biblical significance? As we have seen, it clearly foreshadows the coming totalitarian system the Antichrist will institute in the end times. But does the Bible have anything specific to say about China's role in the end times?

THE ALIGNMENT OF NATIONS

The dramatic emergence of China from a backward communist nation to an economic and military juggernaut is stunning and is leading the way toward the great reset. For students of Bible prophecy, this should come as no surprise because it dovetails with the biblical alignment of nations in the end times. The Bible predicts that world power in the end times will be divided into four main geographical regions. This alignment of nations is delineated according to the four directions on the compass in their relationship to the nation of Israel. The king of the north is Russia (Rosh), joined by Turkey (Meshech, Tubal, Gomer, and Togarmah) and Iran (Persia) (Daniel 11:40; Ezekiel 38:1–6). The southern power, or king of the south, includes the modern Islamic nations of Egypt, Libya (Put), and Sudan (Cush) (Daniel 11:40; Ezekiel 38). The western quadrant includes the kingdom of the Antichrist—consolidated in the reunited Roman Empire. The nations east of the Euphrates River, called the kings from the east, invade the Middle East in the end times (Revelation 16:12–14). Bible prophecy teachers have long maintained that China would be the driving force behind the great eastern power bloc. Current events in China strikingly foreshadow the biblical predictions for the kings from the east.

Three key biblical prophecies are often cited with reference to China's prophetic role.

IS CHINA REFERENCED IN DANIEL 11?

First, many point to Daniel 11. Daniel 11:36 leaps across the centuries and pictures a king who engages in a military conflict with the king of the south and the king of the north. This king is the head of the Revived Roman Empire, the final Antichrist, who by this point has invaded Israel and engaged in a mop-up operation in North Africa in the land of the king of the south.

The prophecy in Daniel 11:44 says, "But then news from the east and the north will alarm him, and he will set out in great anger to destroy and obliterate many" (NLT). While we are not given every detail, many prophecy scholars believe this "news from the east" prophesies a military invasion from the Far East. Although this is possible, remember that when the Antichrist receives this news, he will be in North Africa, so the area to the north and east is Israel. Therefore, this probably refers to an insurrection in Israel that the Antichrist will go forth to quell, not an invasion from the kings from the east.

AN ARMY OF 200 MILLION

Two important passages in Revelation, namely, 9:13–21 and 16:12–16, are also cited as evidence that one of the large armies employed in the final world conflict will be a military force of great power from China. The first hint is found in Revelation 9, where the apostle John said,

> Then the sixth angel blew his trumpet, and I heard a voice speaking from the four horns of the gold altar that stands in the presence of God. And the voice said to the sixth angel who held the trumpet, "Release the four angels who are bound at the great Euphrates River." Then the four angels who had been prepared for this hour and day and month and year were turned loose to kill one-third of all the people on earth. I heard the size of their army, which was 200 million mounted troops. (vv. 13–16 NLT)

The most staggering aspect of this prophecy is the size of the army, which is calculated to be two hundred thousand or two hundred million. Never in military history has there been an army even close to this size. The total number of troops under arms in World War II on both sides of the war was never more than fifty million. The Roman army in the first century consisted of twenty-five legions, or about 125,000 soldiers with an auxiliary army of about the same size.[17] Some have estimated that when the apostle John penned these words in AD 95, the population of the entire world was not over 200 million. For this reason, many are tempted to spiritualize the number or take it as a round number, signifying a huge number, but there is no signal in the text that the number is used in any way other than literal.

The passage goes on to describe the character and cataclysmic impact of this army that wipes out one-third of the world's population in the ensuing struggle:

And this is how I saw in the vision the horses and those who sat on them: the riders had breastplates the color of fire and of hyacinth and of brimstone; and the heads of the horses are like the heads of lions; and out of their mouths proceed fire and smoke and brimstone. A third of mankind was killed by these three plagues, by the fire and the smoke and the brimstone which proceeded out of their mouths. For the power of the horses is in their mouths and in their tails; for their tails are like serpents and have heads, and with them they do harm. (vv. 17–19)

A good number of prophecy scholars believe that the most reasonable explanation of this prophecy, related as it is to the great river Euphrates, is that the army rises from the Far East and crosses the Euphrates River to participate in the final war of Armageddon in the land of Israel. The reference to a huge army and the Euphrates River is often correlated with Revelation 16, which also mentions "the kings from the east" and the Euphrates River. Revelation 9 and 16 are the only two references to the Euphrates River in Revelation, and the entire New Testament.

The statement that it is prepared for an "hour and day and month and year" to slay one-third of humanity simply means that the army is especially prepared for the day of battle and highlights that God is in sovereign control of the timing (Revelation 9:15).

While it is possible to interpret the army of two hundred million in Revelation 9 as a reference to China and other nations east of the Euphrates, it is better to understand it as referring to a massive demonic army that will be unleashed in the end times to wreak havoc on the earth. Two points support this view.

First, the preceding context, the fifth trumpet judgment, is clearly a demonic invasion of the earth (demons symbolized as locusts). Since the fifth and sixth trumpet judgments form a unit as the first two of three "woes" (Revelation 8:13), it is best to view the sixth trumpet as a demonic army as well. Second, fire and brimstone are associated with hell four times in Revelation (14:10–11; 19:20; 20:10; 21:8).

THE KINGS FROM THE EAST

A third biblical reference that probably does relate to China in the end times is found in the sixth bowl judgment described in Revelation 16:12, which says, "The sixth angel poured out his bowl on the great river, the Euphrates; and its water was dried up, so that the way would be prepared for the kings from the east."

Revelation 16:14 reveals that this advance is part of a worldwide gathering of "the kings of the whole world, to gather them together for the war of the great day of God, the Almighty." Revelation 16:16 reveals that the geographical focal point of the gathering is Armageddon (Heb., Har-Magedon), which is Mount Megiddo in northern Israel that overlooks a huge valley known as the Valley of Armageddon, the Valley of Jezreel, or the Plain of Esdraelon. This valley is about ten miles wide and thirty-five miles long.

The clearest, most convincing explanation for understanding "the kings from the east" (16:12) is to take the passage literally. The kings from the east, literally "of the sun rising," refers to nations that originate east of the Euphrates.

Interpreted literally, Revelation 16 provides an important piece of information concerning the final world conflict. According to this chapter, the invasion from the east commences with an act of God in drying up the Euphrates River. This miraculous drying up of the Euphrates permits easy access for the massive army of China and its eastern allies upon the land of Israel.

The Euphrates River is referenced a total of nineteen times in the Old Testament and twice in the New Testament. Genesis 15:18 points to the Euphrates River as the eastern boundary of the land promised to Abraham and his descendants, the nation of Israel. Thus, crossing the Euphrates River from east to west is tantamount to invading the promised land.

One final question concerning China: Why would China, and possibly other nations from east of the Euphrates, such as India, move into Israel in the end times? The Bible never says specifically why the kings of the east make their move. Some believe it will be to oppose the forces of the Antichrist, who will be dominating the world. They believe this will be the final showdown of east versus west. But since the armies are gathered to Armageddon by demonic spirits sent out by Satan and the Antichrist, it appears that China's final great invasion is to join the forces of the Antichrist in a final great battle to crush the Jewish people and secure the land of Israel once and for all.

Much more could be said about the Armageddon campaign, but the final act of this drama will climax when Christ interrupts this conflict with his second coming to earth. He will destroy the Antichrist and all the armies gathered at Armageddon (Revelation 19:11–21).

PAVING THE WAY

China intends to dominate the world and even outer space in the twenty-first century. Its churning economic engine shows no signs of diminishing or even slowing. Its military hegemon is aggressive and growing. Its iron-fisted control over its citizens is tightening. Its part in the great reset is pacesetting.

In China, as in other parts of the world, the stage is being set for the final drama in which the Antichrist will expand the authoritarian system to total global control, and the kings from the east will fulfill their important role in end-time events.

SIX

AMERICA AT DUSK

The world has seen its share of mighty nations and empires. Some of them are portrayed and prophesied in Scripture—Egypt, Assyria, Babylon, Medo-Persia, Greece, and Rome. In this book, we looked briefly at Russia and more extensively at China and its role in Bible prophecy. But what about America, arguably the world's greatest superpower and force of freedom on the planet? What part does America play in the end times? What is its role in this coming global reset? There are multiple theories regarding if or how America is prophesied in Scripture.[1] What should concern us more, however, is if and how America is falling under God's judgment, and whether America can be saved. That's because even once-great civilizations and countries fall, and a time comes when they simply no longer exist.

Among historians, some believe past civilizations have come to an end because of a failure to adapt to new challenges and surroundings. Others, they observe, fall because of the tyranny of despots, revolutions, or through being conquered by stronger nations. Some, however, remain a mystery as to why they eventually ceased to exist.

The great British historian Arnold Toynbee offered an additional theory, adding that some civilizations die from suicide, not by murder.[2]

Essentially, Toynbee asserted that this death of a nation is brought on by a gradually intensifying self-inflicted wound, one that eventually proves fatal. But where is God in all this?

What part, if any, does God play in the death of a civilization or people group? Are there any biblical principles that speak to the rise or collapse of countries? Most people are familiar with God's covenant relationship with Israel, but what about the rest of the world's nations? Are there any specific agreements he has with them? Any particular expectations he has concerning pagan, secular, or Christian nations? What does he expect from Russia, Switzerland, India, or Guatemala? And what about America? Do we get a pass because we were founded upon Judeo-Christian ethics? Or perhaps because we fought and defeated other evil empires that would threaten freedom worldwide? Does our alliance with Israel preserve us somehow? In attempting to answer these questions, it would be easier to simply read the headlines or form opinions based on America's political and moral climate alone. But a better source, and question, is, "What does the Bible say?" To accurately address this, we must look at what God expects of humankind in general, for all nations are little more than the collective expressions of its people.

Scripture gives us concrete truths concerning every person on planet Earth, regardless of race, religion, or country of origin:

1. They are made in the image of God (Genesis 1:26).
2. They have moral conscience (Romans 2:14–15).

3. They are responsible before God (Romans 1:20).
4. God will judge each person based on their response to him (John 3:18, 36; Romans 2:5–11, 16).

Let's unpack each of these a bit further.

1. MADE IN THE IMAGE OF GOD

Let Us make man in Our image. . . . (Genesis 1:26)

Much has been written about what this "image" signifies. We can be certain that it does not mean all people are guaranteed heaven simply because they are born a human being. Salvation is for those who *believe*, not just for those who have been *born*. It is true that we all are God's creations, but not all of us are his children.

Many theologians and trusted Bible scholars believe being made in God's image has to do with his "communicable attributes," or those characteristics that are transferable from him to us. Like God, we possess intellect, emotion, and will. We therefore can think, feel, and choose like he does. Others say the image of God also includes the capacity for relationship and that we are moral beings (i.e., designed to respond positively to righteousness and negatively to sin).

2. MORAL CONSCIOUSNESS FROM GOD

For when Gentiles who do not have the Law do instinctively the things of the Law, these, not having the Law, are a law

> to themselves, in that they show the work of the Law writ-
> ten in their hearts, their conscience bearing witness and
> their thoughts alternately accusing or else defending them.
> (Romans 2:14–15)

Another aspect of humanity is that we possess an innate real-
ization of good and evil. This answers the question of why every
culture, regardless of era or exposure to Judeo-Christian values,
nevertheless still upholds basic moral values. These values are
complementary to, if not exactly like, those outlined in Scripture
and the Ten Commandments. Even pagan cultures adhere to a
fundamental set of moral standards, though not always consistently over time. Within every civilization throughout recorded
history, there has existed some elemental sense of justice, com-
passion, honesty, and morality (right and wrong). This inward
sense is a part of what Scripture calls "conscience." And God put
it there.

Conscience is like a built-in radar detection device, telling
you the difference between right and wrong, good and evil. It is a
part of your basic operating system and comes preloaded in every
human. And those same conscience-bearing humans also make
up cultures, governments, and civilizations. So, as the humans
go, so the countries go. More about that conscience in a bit.

3. RESPONSIBLE BEFORE GOD (ROMANS 1:20)

In addition to the internal witness of morality, Scripture states
that God has also placed *external* evidence of his existence and
character.

For the wrath of God is revealed from heaven against all ungodliness and unrighteousness of men who suppress the truth in unrighteousness, *because that which is known about God is evident within them; for God made it evident to them.* For since the creation of the world His invisible attributes, His eternal power and divine nature, have been clearly seen, being understood through what has been made, *so that they are without excuse.* (Romans 1:18–20, emphasis added)

Several important truths jump out in this passage. First, God has intentionally and purposefully provided credible evidence of himself as Creator to every person. Second, they know it, "for God made it evident to them." He has not left himself without a witness. Third, creation is God's primary external witness of himself to humankind: "since the creation of the world His *invisible attributes,* His *eternal power* and *divine nature,* have been clearly seen, being understood through what has been made" (Romans 1:20, emphasis added).

Without uttering a word, God has communicated volumes to humanity concerning himself (Psalm 19:1–4). Job said that the beasts, birds, and fish declare that God is Creator (Job 12:7–9). Therefore, if the animal creation understands this, shouldn't the crown of his handiwork also acknowledge that in God's "hand is the life of every living thing, and the breath of all mankind" (Job 12:10)?

Fourth, every person is responsible to God. Therefore, he accepts no excuses for not acknowledging him (Romans 1:20). This clear revelation of God to humankind is plain, simple, obvious, natural, and undeniable. In other words, it's "going to be on the test."

4. ACCOUNTABLE BEFORE GOD (JOHN 3:18, 36; ROMANS 1:18, 20; 2:5-11, 16)

He who believes in Him is not judged; he who does not believe has been judged already, because he has not believed in the name of the only begotten Son of God. (John 3:18)

He who believes in the Son has eternal life; but he who does not obey the Son will not see life, but the wrath of God abides on him. (John 3:36)

God will judge individuals and nations based on their response to this revelation of himself to them. This particular judgment is delivered both temporally and eternally, or now and at the final judgment. And what initiates God's wrath against men and nations? Romans 1:18 gives us the answer—ungodly and unrighteous "men who suppress the truth in unrighteousness." To suppress means to ignore, put down, quench, smother, censor, or put out. In short, it is a conscious denial of God's reality, or existence, his role as Creator, and his right to rule in our lives and in the world. It is a willful refusal to "honor Him as God" (Romans 1:21).

But why? Why do people, and nations, ignore God and push him away? Again, the answer is found right here in the passage. According to Romans 1:21, acknowledging God's existence and role as Creator naturally leads to honoring him as God, or submitting ourselves to him as his subjects. To agree with creation, conscience, and Scripture is to lose all rights and ownership to our own lives, something that dangerously threatens self and is diametrically opposed to self-love, self-rule, and self-worship. It means his law, standards, morality, truths, and values trump our own. It means we subject ourselves to his objective truth instead of operating in our own truth. Make no mistake, the sin nature understands all too well what it means to acknowledge God, that it will have to die and be dethroned. And the majority of humanity would simply rather not do that.

It is true that God has given us the freedom to deny him and even to excommunicate him from our culture. We can remove him and his Word from government, schools and universities, the courts, and even the town square. That is a choice we are given. However, there is no freedom given regarding the *consequences* of those choices, which are devastating. One of those consequences is the revelation of God's "wrath."

So, what is the "wrath of God" that is revealed when an individual or nation rejects him and suppresses his truth? Paul outlined seven progressive penalties for both people and nations who fail to respond positively toward God's revelation of himself to them.

DARKNESS (ROMANS 1:21)

For even though they knew God, they did not honor Him as God or give thanks, but they became futile in their speculations, and their foolish heart was *darkened*. (emphasis added)

Without God as the explanation for all there is, humanity is left on their own to figure it out. Unfortunately, without God in the equation, we can never come to the correct conclusion about life and the origin of humankind. God is the only true source of light and truth (John 1:4, 10; 14:6; 1 John 1:5). Therefore, when disconnected from him, people are left in total darkness. And in the darkness, cut off from any light source, they have only their own darkened minds to use in trying to make sense of the world. As a result, their speculations are, by definition, "futile" (Romans 1:21). Like a blind man in a maze or a person lost in the jungle without a compass, it is simply an exercise in futility. The word "speculations" in this verse refers to self-based and self-biased reasoning. In other words, their ideas are simply bouncing back and forth in their tiny, limited, darkened minds. Like a toddler attempting quantum physics, it is a useless, pointless exercise, leading nowhere. All that is produced are empty human ideas but no truth. Out of this futile, darkened state, lies such as evolution are manufactured and propagated. And without God's truth in their minds, humans are left to fill them with other "truths" peddled by culture, Satan, and their own deceitful hearts (Jeremiah 17:9).

DELUSION (ROMANS 1:22-23)

The ironic effect of this darkness is that, though their ideas, values, beliefs, and philosophies are infantile and miss the truth by miles, people nevertheless think themselves somehow erudite because of them. Self-deceit now descends on their minds, convincing them not only of the veracity of their propositions but also of their nobility. In short, they proclaim themselves to be "wise" (Gr. *sophos*, "sophisticated"). And though degrees, accolades, and recognition may follow such persons, this is simply a thin veneer, as God proclaims them to be "fools" (Romans 1:22). For who are fools but the people who think themselves smarter than God?

The word Paul used here for "fool" is *moros*, which means "dull, sluggish, or stupid." This same Greek word was later employed by psychologist Henry Goddard, who in 1910 invented the word *moron* from it, referring to one who suffered from intellectual disabilities.[3] Believing our values and "personal truths" outrank God's truly makes us all morons.

Already we can see the awful consequences of rejecting God's truth, as people's brains and ability to reason are showing signs of deterioration and decay.

But something is also beginning to happen to people's consciences at this stage. According to Paul, the conscience also grows dull with persistent rejection of God. As people reject the Creator and the evidence he has graciously provided, their consciences become "seared . . . as with a branding iron" (1 Timothy 4:2). A branding iron's burn produces a callus, which makes the scar insensitive to touch. At this stage, people even begin reimagining who or what God is, choosing to begin worshiping and venerating the creation instead of the Creator.

DIVINE DELUSION (2 THESSALONIANS 2:10–12)

In 2 Thessalonians Paul wrote that in the last days, unbelievers will not only be deceived by the devil and his miracles but also suffer under a divine delusion sent by God himself. Why does this happen? Is it because God is unloving or unwilling to forgive? Is it because he is cruel or unjust? No, it happens because "they did not receive the love of the truth so as to be saved" (2:10). In other words, they consciously rejected the reality concerning God and his Son that would have brought salvation to them. Therefore, he not only delivers them over to Satan's deceptions but also further blinds their hearts and minds with a supernatural stupor as well. Paul called it a "deluding influence" that results in them believing what is false (2:11).

Rejecting God's truth is a very serious thing and places individuals on thin ice. However, *continued* rejection, especially during the days leading up to the tribulation, breaks that ice, and people fall through into the icy waters of total deception and destruction. Their unbelief and stubborn refusal to believe is like systematically cutting through their own life-saving rope that leads to the surface. It is the epitome of self-hate and self-destruction.

Further, those deluded souls, because of their ongoing unbelief, will even be prevented by God from believing in Christ. Can you envision a more terrifying place to be in life? There is a threshold a person can cross from which there is no return. This is similar to what God did to Pharaoh after Pharaoh hardened his own heart (Romans 9:17–18).[4] When God hardens a person's heart, there is no longer any possibility of repentance. It is at this point, practically speaking, that their destiny is sealed and their doom ensured. Only death and damnation await them. This, then, is the future for all those who suffer deceit and delusion during the tribulation period. And the purpose? "In order that they all may be judged who did not believe the truth, but took pleasure in wickedness" (2 Thessalonians 2:12). They will be convinced of Satan's miracles, believing every lie he tells, the greatest being that his Antichrist is God in human flesh.

DESIRE (ROMANS 1:24-25)

Therefore God gave them over in the lusts of their hearts to impurity, so that their bodies would be dishonored among them. For they exchanged the truth of God for a lie, and worshiped and served the creature rather than the Creator, who is blessed forever. Amen.

At this advanced stage of judgment, it would appear that freedom among men and nations is expanding. The more we remove God, the more liberty we seem to have to do what we want, right? But according to Paul, just the opposite occurs. The phrase "God gave them over" is the Greek verb *paradidomi* and is a judicial term used when a judge hands a prisoner over to his sentence. He is not headed to freedom but rather to prison.

The word "lust" refers to "passionate desire" and in this context signifies sexual "impurity," a term elsewhere associated with illicit sexual activity (Romans 6:19; 2 Corinthians 12:21; Galatians 5:19; Ephesians 4:19; 5:3; Colossians 3:5; 1 Thessalonians 4:7). Revelation 9:21 prophesies there will be a rampant explosion of sexual immorality (*porneia*) in the last days.

In America, our standards regarding sex have continued to plummet. According to Dr. David Jeremiah, "In January 2016, the Internet's largest online pornography site released its annual statistics. On just this website, in just one year—2015—consumers watched 4,392,486,580 hours of pornography."[5]

Converted into years, that is 500,000 years of watching porn. No one would deny that we are a society obsessed with sex. In fact, we are saturated in it. And it is not just "regular" porn,

Jeremiah said. "According to a CNN article, the United States is home to more commercial child porn websites than anywhere else on earth."[6]

Though in past generations we may have said, "Anything goes" or "If it feels good, do it," today's catchphrase would be "Follow your heart" or "What does your heart tell you?" Again, the subtle deception of the human heart is to be convinced of one's own freedom to pursue desires, when in reality doing so is a telltale sign that God is letting go.

Before we proceed, let us acknowledge that these are not happy thoughts or comforting truths, and explaining them gives us no pleasure. However, this is God's truth and reality. He would prefer that individuals and countries be who they were created to be—worshipers of God—but we have chosen a different path. Hopefully, these shocking truths will enlighten our minds and motivate our hearts toward Jesus.

DEVIANCE (ROMANS 1:26–27)

Sin, self, and society are not merely content to explore the natural desires of humanity in illegitimate ways. Rather, they soon become bored with "traditional sexual sin," exchanging it for something out of the natural realm of men and women.

> For this reason God gave them over to degrading passions; for
> their women exchanged the natural function for that which
> is unnatural, and in the same way also the men abandoned
> the natural function of the woman and burned in their desire
> toward one another, men with men committing indecent acts

and receiving in their own persons the due penalty of their error. (Romans 1:26–27)

Notice again the repeating of the phrase "God gave them over." This time he gave them over to a passion that was "degrading" to them. This word means to strip them of honor, or to rob them of their intrinsic value or worth. In this sense, homosexuality is ultimately an expression of self-hate in that it steals from the individual the value they would have found in the beautiful design and role God originally created for them.

Also observe that Paul began by addressing lesbianism first, not male homosexuality. This is intentional. Theologian Charles Hodge explained why he believed this was so: "Paul first refers to the degradation of females among the heathen, because they are always the last to be affected in the decay of morals, and their corruption is therefore proof that all virtue is lost."[7]

Women have been called the conscience of a culture, whereas, typically, men more readily respond and succumb to their lustful desires, especially in the area of sexuality. So if women are ruined, we can be confident that men have long since been the same way.

According to Paul here, there is nothing whatsoever natural about lesbianism. Not only does it flatly contradict basic biology, nature, and civilization, but also the created order designed by God (Genesis 1:26–27). No one is *born* a homosexual any more than they are born a thief, drunkard, or swindler. We are all, however, born sinners, and each one of us eventually chooses our own areas of sinful expression (Mark 7:20–23; Romans 3:23).

Interestingly, Paul used the word *pathos* (translated "passions") in Romans 1:26 when speaking of the woman's homosexual desire. This word links those passions to feelings of intimacy and romanticism, another deception convincing women that what they are feeling for the same sex is real and natural. No one would deny that sexual desire is a potent narcotic. And while under the influence, we can easily begin trusting in what our sinful bodies and darkened minds are telling us.

Paul next turned his attention to male homosexuality, stating that to arrive at this attraction or practice, one must "abandon" (lit., "to send away") the natural, God-given desire for women and replace it with a fiery desire for same-sex relationships. We see this same level of burning desire among the homosexual men of Sodom. Even after being supernaturally struck blind by the two angels, so great was their insatiable desire to gang rape God's angels, they actually "wearied themselves" trying to locate Lot's doorway (Genesis 19:5, 11).

Paul elsewhere condemned homosexuality, stating that no homosexual will "enter the kingdom of heaven" (1 Corinthians 6:9). Again, sobering, uncomfortable truths. Here in Romans 1:27, he added a further, more earthly consequence to same-sex activity among men: "receiving in their own persons the due penalty of their error." This appears to be referencing sexually transmitted disease, which was prevalent and known in ancient cultures.[8] According to the Centers for Disease Control and Prevention (CDC), homosexual men account for 83 percent of syphilis cases in the United States.[9]

As a nation, our tolerance for these types of sexual sins has widened. Parents now encourage their children upon the revelation that they are gay. Some parents even promote this deviance on their children from childhood, refusing to refer to the child by a certain gender until he or she "chooses for themself."

Homosexuality is accepted today like traditional relationships were in previous generations. Gay rights activists would applaud this "progress." And with the 2015 case of *Obergefell v. Hodges*, the Supreme Court of the United States voted 5–4 to redefine the concept of marriage by declaring homosexual relationships to be considered legitimate.

Christians, however, claim God alone designed and defines what marriage is, not human courts, public sentiment, or popular vote (Genesis 2:21–24; Mark 10:6–8).

Ancient Jewish rabbis wrote that "societal recognition of such homosexual relationships [marriages] will bring upon that society extreme forms of Divine punishment," asserting that "when [such] sin is no longer recognized as sin by a society . . . that society loses its right to existence—like the generation of the Flood."[10] In other words, the more homosexuality we condone, the more condemnation we invite.

Before moving on to the next stage of God's abandonment wrath, we want to be very clear in declaring that God loves homosexuals very much, including all those who struggle with sexual identity issues. Jesus died for their sins, too, and his desire is for them to call upon him for salvation so that they can discover their intended identity in Jesus Christ. And yet those who continue resisting the clear call to help and hope through Jesus will, as this passage declares, be given over by God to their own desires.

DEPRAVITY (ROMANS 1:28–31)

Just how far down into the depths of sin can humans go? We are about to find out. The next level of judgment describes the third and final level of abandonment wrath this side of eternity.

And just as they did not see fit to acknowledge God any longer, God gave them over to a depraved mind, to do those things which are not proper, being filled with all unrighteousness, wickedness, greed, evil; full of envy, murder, strife, deceit, malice; they are gossips, slanderers, haters of God, insolent, arrogant, boastful, inventors of evil, disobedient to parents, without understanding, untrustworthy, unloving, unmerciful. (Romans 1:28–31)

Space does not permit me to fully unpack all the sins Paul listed, but we can get a good idea of what they mean by understanding the umbrella phrase, "depraved mind." Again, the same judicial sentence is pronounced upon them here. The word *depraved* literally means to "fail the test." It was used in the first century in the world of metallurgy to describe metal impurities that rose to the top and were thrown away as useless or worthless. A depraved mind is one that has "failed" and been rejected by God and deemed "worthless." Put another way, the mind that continually rejects God is, at some point, then fully rejected by him. God is declaring to this person (and nation), "You fully belong to *you and your sin* now. I'm out."

A depraved mind is no longer affected by God's influence, as that influence has now been removed. The mind signifies the reasoning and thinking processes. Therefore, this depraved mind belongs to someone whose reasoning and thinking processes no longer function on a rational, healthy level. The darkness that descended on this mind upon his rejection of God as Creator and Ruler is now complete. All consciousness regarding God, good, and godliness has been depleted from the mind. And because nature abhors a void, in its place comes flooding a torrent of wickedness. Into a bottomless pit spirals sin out of control. This was pandemic during the days of Noah (Genesis 6:5).

It is nothing short of moral and spiritual insanity.

DESTRUCTION (ROMANS 1:32)

Paul concluded the abandonment protocol by describing the ultimate fate of those who suffer this judgment:

> Although they know the ordinance of God, that those who practice such things are worthy of death, they not only do the same, but also give hearty approval to those who practice them. (Romans 1:32)

The participants in these sins are the promoters of them as well.

They do not merely practice them but also give hearty approval to others who practice them. Today we have a broad assortment of celebrations and gatherings with the sole purpose of allowing participants to proudly parade their sin before God and a watching world. In America we now have an entire month of the year (June) set aside to recognize and celebrate homosexual "pride." In 2015 #ShoutYourAbortion went viral, with a website subsequently devoted to help women celebrate the murder of their unborn children, even helping them throw parties for that purpose. What have we become?

Tolerance. Acceptance. Justification. Support. Legalization. Celebration. Exaltation.

It seems we have lost the ability to blush at our sin, much less weep over it.

This spirit is reminiscent of the stern and sobering words of the prophets, "Woe to those who call evil good, and good evil; who substitute darkness for light and light for darkness; who substitute bitter for sweet and sweet for bitter!" (Isaiah 5:20).

> For My people are foolish,
> They know Me not;
> They are stupid children
> And have no understanding.
> They are shrewd to do evil,
> But to do good they do not know." (Jeremiah 4:22)

And as Paul later wrote,

> "There is none righteous, not even one;
> There is none who understands,
> There is none who seeks for God;
> All have turned aside, together they have become
>   useless;
> There is none who does good,
> There is not even one."
> "Their throat is an open grave,
> With their tongues they keep deceiving,"
> "The poison of asps is under their lips";
> "Whose mouth is full of cursing and bitterness";
> "Their feet are swift to shed blood,
> Destruction and misery are in their paths,
> And the path of peace they have not known."

"There is no fear of God before their eyes."
(Romans 3:10–18)

So, where does all this lead? In a word, "death" (Romans 1:32; 6:23) and, ultimately, spiritual separation from God forever in the lake of fire (Revelation 20:11–15).

Encountering these bold realities and truths from God's Word, we should be a nation on our knees repenting and begging God for his forgiveness because of our sin. Instead, we as a nation continue "storing up wrath for [ourselves] in the day of wrath and revelation of the righteous judgment of God, who will render to each person according to his deeds" (Romans 2:5–6). According to what we have seen in Romans 1, it seems clear that we are currently under God's abandonment judgment. But how long will God wait before he drops the full fury of his wrath upon us as a nation?

This highlights the spiritual law of cause and effect. The cause is humanity's rejection of God and his truth. The effect is darkened hearts (Romans 1:21), empty speculations (v. 21), the delusion that they are wiser than God (v. 22), the worship of creation (vv. 23, 25), immoral sexual relations (v. 24), homosexual and lesbian lifestyles (vv. 26–27), depravity of mind (v. 28), and the pursuit of every kind of improper practice (vv. 28–32).

And with each step deeper into self and sin, God sentences them to a deeper abyss of divine abandonment. The apostle John highlighted this natural propensity for evil. He wrote, "This is the judgment, that the Light [Jesus] has come into the world, and men loved the darkness rather than the Light, for their deeds were evil" (John 3:19).

This lends even further justification for God declaring that "they are without excuse" (Romans 1:20). It is also why God declared (concerning the tribulation generation and the judgments he will pour out on them), "They deserve it" (Revelation 16:6). This is why, on the day of the great white throne judgment, God will accept no excuse or entertain any arguments as to someone's reasons for not acknowledging him or submitting to his rule in their lives. It simply becomes a matter of, "Did you know my Son, and is your name in the Book of Life?" (Matthew 7:23; Revelation 20:11–15).

Is it possible that we as a country have reached a point of no return? Have our repeated spiritual, political, and moral choices caused us to be given over to slavery to our own sins? Is it too late?

Are we like the crew of the Apollo 13 mission, who after near tragedy were able to recover and make it safely home?

Or does the *Titanic* more accurately describe us, irreparably damaged and headed into the icy waters of oblivion?

Is our mission now one of saving America or of saving *Americans*? Our democracy perhaps can be saved, but can America's soul?

Like the Amorites, is our iniquity now "complete" (Genesis 15:16)? Is the final downfall of our once great country really approaching? As America continues to weaken as a world superpower, we are becoming more sympathetic to a global governance model, especially in the context of current worldwide crises and those prophesied to come.

We do not see America specifically mentioned in Bible prophecy. Therefore, America probably will not emerge as a major player in the last days. What we can say for sure is that though it clearly seems the sun of God's favor is setting on America, and we are quickly approaching the twilight hour, we have still not yet reached "dusk."

The great nineteenth-century hymnist Amy Carmichael wrote, "We shall have all eternity to celebrate [our] victories, but we have only the few hours before sunset in which to win them."[11]

The time is short. The hour is late. But our calling is sure. We are clearly experiencing the later stages of moral decline and ongoing influence of the proposed global reset, whose culmination the world could witness soon. Therefore, *now* is the time to reach and disciple those in America so that when she eventually does go down, we can say with confidence we did all we could to help others make it to safety.

SEVEN

WHAT ARE WE WAITING FOR?

While on a trip to London several years ago, I (Jeff) took a group of students to see the classic play *Les Misérables*. Having spent a week of ministering to churches in rural England, I planned our last few days in England to be spent shopping and sightseeing in historic London. Not being an avid fan of plays, and in particular musicals, I was skeptical of attending the performance. But, after all, it was the world's longest-running musical. And my wife convinced me.

Having prepurchased our tickets, we arrived at the famed Palace Theatre, and we were shown to our seats. As we chatted and browsed through the printed program, I surveyed the beautiful theater, observing its Victorian splendor, including hand-carved archways and ornate balcony railings. It was nearing showtime, and the enthusiasm from the packed house swelled with each passing minute. Then, at 8:30 p.m., the room suddenly grew quiet, like the calm before a storm. All eyes turned forward in anticipation. Backstage the actors stood ready, having previously prepared for that moment each night when they made their debut. They had already been through hair, makeup, and wardrobe. The necessary props were in place. The set lighting was fixed. Audio engineers had carefully hidden microphones in the actors' clothing and on stage. The background scenery was complete and ready to be revealed. All of it was prescripted and planned out beforehand. Nothing was left to do but to strike up the orchestra and raise the curtain. Having never been to a play of this caliber before, I did not know what to expect. But as we reached those final seconds before showtime, I, too, became strangely filled with expectation. It was "showtime." And the only question on my mind was, *What are they waiting for?*

Human history can be compared to a play written and directed by the hand of Providence. Act 1 was creation; act 2, the fall; act 3, the flood; and so on. For some time now, we have found ourselves in the latter acts of God's historical narrative. This "church age," or age of grace, seems to have lingered for longer than any of us might have preferred. We know from Scripture what the next act will entail but not when the curtain will fall, only to rise in Revelation. This prolonged period has prompted scoffers to ridicule the Lord and his bride concerning end-times prophecies. At the same time, believers are also asking, "What is God waiting for?"

Fair enough.

THE STAGE IS SET

As we survey the Bible, we see hundreds of previous prophecies concerning Jesus' first coming fulfilled—literally and precisely—as they were written. Here are just ten of them:

- His birthplace (Micah 5:2; Matthew 2:1–6)
- His genealogy (Genesis 12:3; 21:12; 28:14; 49:10; 2 Samuel 7:12–16; Isaiah 11:1; Matthew 1:1–17)
- His virgin birth (Isaiah 7:14; Matthew 1:21–23)
- His arrival in Jerusalem (Daniel 9:24–25; Zechariah 9:9; Luke 19:37–42)
- His forerunner (Isaiah 40:3; Malachi 3:1; Luke 3:2–6)
- His betrayal (Psalm 41:9; Zechariah 11:12; Matthew 26:14–15; John 13:26)
- His suffering (Psalm 22:16; Isaiah 53:4–6; Zechariah 12:10; John 19:34; 20:25)
- His death for sinners (Isaiah 53:8, 11–12; Mark 10:45; John 19:30)
- His burial (Isaiah 53:9; Matthew 27:57–60)
- His resurrection (Psalm 16:10; Matthew 28:6; Acts 2:31–32)

It is reasonable to conclude that since all past prophecies were fulfilled at his first coming, all future prophecies related to his return will also be fulfilled in like manner. When speaking of the future coming of the Lord, the apostle Paul frequently used the word *parousia*, meaning "presence, arrival, or coming." In ancient times, the word was used to describe the arrival of a king. In the New Testament, it is used twenty-four times, seventeen of them referring to the future return of Jesus. Ten of those uses refer to the rapture, while seven of them picture the Second Coming. Though the rapture and the Second Coming are two distinct and separate events, many Bible scholars often view the "coming of the Lord" as one truth, occurring in two *phases*—the rapture and the Second Coming.

At the rapture, Jesus will come *for* his bride, the church (1 Thessalonians 4:13–18), while at the Second Coming, he will return *with* his bride (Revelation 19:11–16).

The rapture will *rescue* believers from God's wrath poured out during the seven-year tribulation (1 Thessalonians 1:10; 5:9; Revelation 3:10), while the Second Coming will occur at the end of that seven-year time of wrath and bring *retribution* to Christ's enemies (2 Thessalonians 2:8; Revelation 19:10–21).

At the rapture, Jesus will come in the air and will be seen only by the church (1 Thessalonians 4:16–17), while at the Second Coming, he will come in the clouds, touch down on earth, and every eye will see him (Daniel 7:13; Zechariah 14:4; Revelation 1:7). Because these two appearances accomplish two different purposes, they cannot be the same event.

Ironically, as the signs of the last days continue to become more obvious, criticism of the rapture has actually increased, even within the church. Unbelievers mock the rapture as apocalyptic religious science fiction, with some even designating a day of the year (May 11) as "Rapture Party Day" to celebrate the failed past predictions of that event.[1] Whether this mocking is real or just another excuse to party is anyone's guess. Admittedly, many misguided individuals have sensationalized the subject of the rapture, creating fear, confusion, and disappointment—and, yes, ridicule.

Nevertheless, this in no way invalidates Scripture's prophecies of such an event. Logically, it is either going to happen or it is not. On this we can all agree. And yet Peter predicted that there will still be those who, even when rationally presented the real truth concerning the coming of the Lord, will deride it, scoff at it, and even satirize it.

Know this first of all, that in the last days mockers will come with their mocking, following after their own lusts, and saying, "Where is the promise of His coming? For ever since the fathers fell asleep, all continues just as it was from the beginning of creation." For when they maintain this, it escapes their notice that by the word of God the heavens existed long ago and the earth was formed out of water and by water, through which the world at that time was destroyed, being flooded with water. But by His word the present heavens and earth are being reserved for fire, kept for the day of judgment and destruction of ungodly men. But do not let this one fact escape your notice, beloved, that with the Lord one day is like a thousand years, and a thousand years like one day. (2 Peter 3:3–8)

There are several substantive truths that Peter wanted us to understand regarding these last days' scoffers:

1. Expect them. "*Know* this" (2 Peter 3:3, emphasis added; see also Jude v. 18).
2. The last days will see an increase in this scoffing activity (2 Peter 3:3).
3. Mockers will attempt to invalidate Bible prophecy by casting doubt on it (2 Peter 3:4): "Where is the promise of His coming?"
4. Their argument will be largely illogical, not factual (2 Peter 3:4): "all continues just as it was from the beginning of creation." In other words, since there was no judgment since creation, there will not be a future one. Their belief in universal uniformity is what drives them. This is the

belief that the laws of nature remain constant and that no outside force (i.e., God) can corrupt that constant.

5. They willingly ignore God's past flood judgment (2 Peter 3:5–7): "It escapes their notice." The evidence of a global flood is literally everywhere on earth, yet they choose to ignore it.

6. Christians must not forget that God is timeless and his promises are sure (2 Peter 3:8).

Sadly, however, among professing believers, the belief in the rapture is also sometimes dismissed as a futuristic fairy tale and misinterpretation of Scripture. Among their arguments is the claim that because the English word *rapture* is not found in the Bible, the doctrine of the rapture also cannot be found. But keep in mind that many core teachings of Christianity are popularly known by English names and descriptions that are nowhere found in Scripture. Words like *Trinity, missions, Great Commission, incarnation, Christmas, Easter,* and even the word *Bible* are not found in any of the sixty-six books of the Bible. This highlights the fact that our belief in a particular doctrine is not substantiated based on the name we use to describe it but on whether the Bible actually teaches it.

Another criticism cast at the rapture is the claim that it is a more *recent* belief and not a doctrine whose roots can be traced to historical Christianity. However, this, too, is a bogus assertion. In one of the earliest extrabiblical writings, the *Didache* (Greek for "teaching"), we find solid evidence of the belief that the Lord could return at any moment (also known as the doctrine of "imminence").

"Be careful how you live. Do not let your lamps be quenched, nor your loins ungirdled, but be ready, for you do not know the hour our Lord will come."[2]

Ultimately, the validity of any doctrine is discovered by simply answering the question "What does the Bible say?" And as we survey the New Testament, multiple scriptures provide solid evidence that the first-century church believed their Lord's return was indeed *imminent*.[3]

WHAT IS THE RAPTURE?

One of those *parousia* (coming, arrival) passages is found in 1 Thessalonians 4. Among the issues troubling the believers at Thessalonica was the end times (i.e., eschatology), specifically, the following: What happens to Christians when they die? Will we see them again? Will we go through the tribulation? Are we currently already in "the day of the Lord"?

Because false teachers had crept into the church and were confusing them concerning the end times, Paul addressed these concerns directly in both 1 and 2 Thessalonians. But in tackling the first question about what happens to believers when they die, he took the opportunity to tell them that they would be reunited with those beloved believers who had either died or been martyred for their faith. And he did this by teaching them about the rapture.

The rapture (also known as the blessed hope, the coming, or the appearing of our Lord) is the event by which Jesus Christ will return for his bride as he promised in John 14:1–3. At this time, he will take her to his Father's house where he has been preparing a place for her.

The English word *rapture* is an English transliteration of a Latin verb (*rapio*, or *rapiemur*). When translating 1 Thessalonians 4:17 from Greek into Latin in the fourth century, the Catholic Church chose this word to represent the original Greek word—*harpazo*. Over time, when speaking of the Lord's coming, the truth found in this verse became known as *rapturo* in Latin. One can easily see how the word *rapture* is derived from that Latin term.

The Greek word *harpazo* means to be "caught up, seized, captured, carried off by force, claimed for oneself, or suddenly snatched away." Luke used this word to describe Philip being "snatched . . . away" and immediately finding himself in another location (Acts 8:39–40). Paul spoke of being "caught up" into the third heaven in 2 Corinthians 12:2. John, in Revelation, referred to Jesus' ascension as him being "caught up to God and to His throne" (Revelation 12:5). Of the fourteen times *harpazo* is used in the New Testament, each time it speaks of someone or something being snatched away by force or seized. Five of those times it means to be caught up to heaven or to be snatched away.[4]

The meaning of this word fits seamlessly with the Jewish wedding custom of Jesus' day. After becoming betrothed to his beloved, the groom would return to his father's house, whereupon he would begin construction or remodeling, to "prepare a place" for his bride. Then, typically six months to a year later, he would return unannounced to snatch his bride away to the marriage ceremony. Though the bride never knew the exact day her betrothed would return, she could discern the general season of his arrival, due to the nature of the betrothal length. Therefore, she had to be ready to leave at any time (imminence) and make sure there was oil in her lamp should he return at night (Matthew 25:1–13).[5]

What can we learn from Paul's teaching regarding the rapture in 1 Thessalonians 4? First, we notice that he was very concerned that those believers did not remain in the dark regarding what was going to take place: "But we do not want you to be uninformed, brethren" (1 Thessalonians 4:13).

This same spirit carried over into his next letter to those Christians: "Now we request you, brethren, with regard to the coming of our Lord Jesus Christ and our gathering together to Him, that you not be quickly shaken from your composure or be disturbed either by a spirit or a message or a letter as if from us, to the effect that the day of the Lord has come" (2 Thessalonians 2:1–2).

The apostle was very intentional about setting the record straight regarding the last days. He wanted them (and us) to be confident concerning future prophetic realities—not to wonder, guess, or be confused or fearful, disturbed, skeptical, unbelieving, or unsure, but rather to *know*—for confidence to reign over confusion. But this was not the first time Paul had covered eschatology with them. After surveying the chronology of the last days' apostasy, the rise of the Antichrist, his character, and his deeds, Paul paused to remind them, "Do you not remember that while I was still with you, I was telling you these things?" (2 Thessalonians 2:5).

This tells us that teaching concerning the end times, rapture, the day of the Lord, and the return of Jesus to the earth was a part of Paul's church-planting curriculum. And why? First, because it is truth. Second, because his readers were potentially living in the time of Jesus' return. And third, because God does not want his children to stay in the dark concerning such things.

WHO WILL PARTICIPATE IN THE RAPTURE?

In 1 Thessalonians 4:14, Paul stated that when the Lord returns, he "will bring with Him those who have fallen asleep in Jesus." This answers the question of where these believers have been since death (in heaven with God). Then Paul pivoted toward us, revealing that "we who are alive and remain until the coming of the Lord" will participate in this event as well (1 Thessalonians 4:15)—as in "all of us." One of the most unsupportable theories regarding the rapture is that only some Christians will be snatched away (i.e., a "partial rapture"). And though there are no specific verses to support such a belief, some continue holding fast to it. They likely do this because they do not quite know how to reconcile professing Christians who have never really lived for Christ and those believers who may not be walking with the Lord at the time of the rapture. They do not believe God will send them to hell, so they create an alternate punishment for them—hell on earth. Their way of solving this problem is for Jesus to leave those "carnal Christians" behind when he comes. It is believed that the shock of being abandoned here by their Lord will lead them to confession and repentance, perhaps in hopes of yet another mini-rapture, just prior to, or sometime during, the tribulation. This would, of course, lead to "multiple raptures."

Again, no scriptural evidence exists for this belief. On the contrary, the Bible indicates that *all* true believers, regardless of their spiritual condition or closeness to the Lord at the moment of his return, will be raptured (1 Corinthians 15:51–52: "we will *all* be changed"; 1 Thessalonians 4:14–15: "we who are alive"). There are no qualifications, contingencies, or exemptions to these verses. If you are truly *in Christ*, you will participate in the rapture, either through returning with him from heaven or by being snatched up alive by him. Further, only *one* future rapture event is mentioned in Scripture, not multiple ones. And last, Jesus paid for and forgave all sins at salvation (Romans 5:1; 8:1; Ephesians 1:7; Colossians 1:14; 2:12–14). Any sin that could keep you from being raptured has already been covered and forgiven by Jesus. The body of Christ is raptured whole, not in parts. There are no "first-class seats" at the rapture. Everybody flies.

HOW WILL THE RAPTURE HAPPEN?

Paul outlined for us a specific chronology of the rapture. First, Jesus will descend from heaven with a "shout" (1 Thessalonians 4:16). This is his first penetration into Earth's atmosphere since he last passed through it at his ascension somewhere between AD 30 and 33 (Luke 24:51–52; Acts 1:9–11; Hebrews 1:1–3). We are not told what Jesus will shout, and this is one of the rapture's mysteries. In fact, the rapture itself was considered a mystery until God revealed it (1 Corinthians 15:51).

Some have suggested this shout will be directed at those bodies in the grave, most of them long since decomposed and disintegrated. Just as he commanded Lazarus to "come forth" (John 11:43), perhaps he will issue the same command of them.

Or it could be a command similar to the invitation given to John, "Come up here" (Revelation 4:1).

Second, the voice of an archangel will be heard. Once again, we are not told what he will say, so we cannot speak with certainty (another mystery). However, considering the wedding narrative that encompasses the rapture, it could be comparable to what the best man of Matthew 25:6 shouted to the bride-to-be: "Behold the bridegroom! Come out to meet him." The identity of this archangel is not known, and we are only told in Scripture who one of them is—Michael (Jude v. 9). However, Daniel does tell us there is more than one of this class of "chief princes" (Daniel 10:13). Since Michael's duties seem tied to national Israel (Daniel 12:1–3), this rapture archangel is perhaps one who has been appointed to specifically watch over the bride.

The next sound believers will hear is "the trumpet of God" (1 Thessalonians 4:16). Paul called this the "last trumpet" in 1 Corinthians 15:52. Some have confused this trumpet with Revelation's seventh trumpet judgment, which occurs around the midpoint of the tribulation or later (Revelation 11:15–19). But this is not a trumpet associated with God's wrath. Rather, it is one that calls the assembly together, much like in Old Testament times (Exodus 19:16–19). Possibly, it is called the "last trumpet" because it signals the end of the church age.

At these commanding, regal sounds, "the dead in Christ will rise first" (1 Thessalonians 4:16). Those who have previously died in Christ have been with the Lord in their spirits since their passing (2 Corinthians 5:8; Philippians 1:23). Now they will be rejoined with their bodies, ones made new, imperishable, immortal, and glorified (1 Corinthians 15:52–53).

Next, we who are alive will be "raptured" (*harpazo*), snatched up by Christ himself, together with those saints' resurrected bodies, to "meet the Lord" (1 Thessalonians 4:17). For as long as we have believed, we have walked by faith, trusting God and believing his promises. However, at this moment, our faith will finally become sight (1 Corinthians 13:12; 2 Corinthians 5:7; 1 John 3:2).

At the rapture, we who are alive will also be changed, our mortal bodies transformed into immortal ones (1 Corinthians 15:51–53). Our spirits will be changed as well. Gone will be the weight and influence of the sin nature, as we will be made like Jesus. Our salvation will be complete at last (Romans 8:29–30; 1 John 3:2). Paul used two phrases in 1 Corinthians 15:52 to describe how quickly this supernatural event and transformation will occur. The first is "in a moment." This Greek word (*atomo*) refers to "that which cannot be divided" or "that which is indivisible." In other words, it is so instantaneous that if it were a timeline, you would be unable to detect the beginning, middle, or end.

The second phrase is "in the twinkling of an eye," generally understood to be the length of time it takes light to refract on the eyeball. Both these Greek words (moment, twinkling) are used only here in Scripture.

So exactly how fast will the rapture occur?

Faster than thought itself.

And yet it is plausible to speculate that we may be able to comprehend what is happening in that moment, as all of our faculties (mind, emotions, body, perception) will be reformatted for a new supernatural, heavenly environment.

WHERE WILL THE RAPTURE OCCUR?

The effects of the rapture will be felt on the earth in two ways. First, graves all over the world will be emptied of their contents. Second, living believers from every nation, tribe, and tongue will instantly disappear, right in front of family members, friends, neighbors, coworkers, classmates, and teammates. This is where the real thrill for us will take place, "in the air," where we will "meet the Lord." As the eighteenth-century hymn writer penned:

> Farewell, vain World, I must be gone,
> I have no Home or stay in Thee;
> I take my Staff, and travel on
> Till I a better World can see.[6]

Following the rapture, "we shall always be with the Lord" (1 Thessalonians 4:17; see also Revelation 4:4–11; 19:14).

WHY WILL THERE BE A RAPTURE?

There appear to be three primary biblical purposes for the rapture:

1. For Jesus to fulfill his promise and receive us and take us to his Father's house (John 14:2–3; 1 Thessalonians 4:17)
2. For us to be transformed and be given our glorified bodies (1 Corinthians 15:51–52; 1 John 3:2)
3. For us to be delivered from God's wrath during the

seven-year tribulation (1 Thessalonians 1:10; 5:9; Revelation 3:10)

WHEN WILL THE RAPTURE TAKE PLACE?

The timing of the rapture is one of the most debated topics in eschatology. At the heart of the matter is the question, precisely *when* will Jesus return for his bride? This, of course, is operating under the assumption that there will be a literal seven-year tribulation as described in Daniel and Revelation. The major views fall under four main categories: pretribulational, midtribulational, prewrath, and post-tribulational.

The pretribulational view asserts that the rapture will happen *before* the time of God's wrath in the tribulation and that his wrath will last the full seven years of that time.

The midtribulational view puts the rapture at three and a half years into the tribulation. Proponents of this view say the wrath poured out in the first three and a half years will not be from God but rather from Satan and man.

The prewrath view says God's wrath will not begin until the seventh trumpet judgment. Therefore, Christians will not be raptured until about three-quarters of the way into the tribulation.

The post-tribulational view states that Christians will endure all of God's judgments (seal, bowl, trumpets) and somehow be preserved through them. Essentially, the church's rapture will occur immediately prior to the second coming of Christ, whereupon God's people quickly mount horses and return to the earth with him.

So, when *will* the wrath of God begin, and will Christians

have to go through any of it? Entire books have been written on the subject, but here are six reasons why we believe the *pretribu-lational* view of the rapture is the most logical and biblical:

1. God's wrath begins in Revelation 6 and continues through chapter 18. Because Jesus (not Satan) is the one who breaks the first seal (6:1), the judgments begin at this time. Revelation 6:2 is when the Antichrist signs his peace treaty, thus officially launching the tribulation (Daniel 9:26).

2. God's wrath toward us was 100 percent satisfied on Jesus at the cross (John 19:30). Therefore, there is no longer any wrath or anger toward God's children (Romans 8:1). To subject his redeemed bride to his fury and anger toward sin would be to denigrate both Christ and his substitu-tionary atonement on our behalf (1 John 2:2).

3. God has promised to spare the church from his coming wrath:

    Wait for His Son from heaven, whom He raised from the dead, that is Jesus, *who rescues us from the wrath to come.* (1 Thessalonians 1:10, emphasis added)

    For God has not destined us for wrath, but for obtaining salvation through our Lord Jesus Christ. (1 Thessalonians 5:9, emphasis added)

    Because you have kept the word of My perseverance, I also will keep you from the hour of testing, that hour which is about to come upon the whole world, to test those who dwell on the earth. (Revelation 3:10)

The context of all three of these passages is the coming day of the Lord (tribulation). "Wrath" here refers to the judgments found in Revelation 6–18. In the Revelation 3 passage, God does not promise to keep us *through* "the hour of testing . . . which is about to come upon the whole world," but rather to keep us *from* that dark hour. The Greek words used ("keep from") are *tereo ek*, which mean to "protect, or guard from" or "remove from." John could easily have said the church would be kept "in" or "through" the tribulation, but he chose the word "from" instead. In other words, the bride will be exempt *from* this coming era of judgment, not be preserved *through* it. Jesus prayed in the garden of Gethsemane to be saved "from" his hour of suffering (John 12:27). In his humanity, he was asking to avoid the cross altogether and to be delivered from it. But because he was not delivered from God's wrath, we will be.

If we are forced to endure any part of the tribulation and God's wrath, then Jesus' words in Revelation 3:10 cannot mean what they plainly appear to mean. It is true that while we are in this world, we will have opposition, persecution, and tribulation (John 15:18–21; 16:33), but there is a vast difference between man's wrath and God's wrath. A stark contrast between tribulation and *the* tribulation.

4. The church is nowhere mentioned in Revelation during the time of the tribulation (Revelation 6–18). The word *church* (Gk. "ecclesia") is used twenty times in Revelation. This is how it breaks down:

   › Nineteen times in chapters 1–3
   › One time in chapter 19

> *Zero* times in chapters 4–18 and 20–22

After the first three chapters, we do not see the bride again until she returns with Christ from heaven at the Second Coming (Revelation 19:7–14).

5. The church is portrayed as being in heaven prior to the beginning of Revelation's judgments. We believe the twenty-four elders of Revelation 4 represent the church, as all are given crowns and clothed in white garments (1 Corinthians 9:25; 1 Thessalonians 2:19; 2 Timothy 4:8; James 1:12; 1 Peter 5:4; Revelation 2:10; 3:11; 4:4, 10; 19:7–8).

6. The purpose of the tribulation precludes the church being involved. According to Scripture, there are two primary purposes for the tribulation. Revelation 3:10 says that "hour which is about to come upon the whole world" is "to test those who dwell on the earth." Clearly, this is a reference to the judgments of Revelation 6 through 18. Second, the seven years are also the fulfillment of the "seventy weeks" of Daniel (Daniel 9:24–27). This is specifically related to national Israel. The church did not participate in the previous sixty-nine weeks prophesied concerning Israel, so there is no reason to believe she will participate in the seventieth.

When seen scripturally, the rapture is both a *romance* and a *rescue*. A story of a promise fulfilled and protection provided. This beautiful doctrine is not meant to divide us but to instill within us confidence (1 Thessalonians 4:13), hope (4:13), and great comfort (4:18).

SO WHAT *ARE* WE WAITING FOR?

Yes, we are waiting. Paul put it this way:

> For our citizenship is in heaven, from which also we eagerly *wait* for a Savior, the Lord Jesus Christ. (Philippians 3:20, emphasis added)

> [We are to be] *looking* for the blessed hope and the appearing of the glory of our great God and Savior, Christ Jesus. (Titus 2:13, emphasis added)

> Everyone who has this hope fixed on Him *purifies* himself, just as He is pure. (1 John 3:3, emphasis added)

Waiting. Looking. Purifying.

Exactly what you would expect a loving bride to do.

So, what is keeping that last trumpet from being blown? In a word, *patience*. As it turns out, we are not the only ones waiting. God waits as well.

"The Lord is not slow about His promise, as some count slowness, but is *patient toward you, not wishing for any to perish but for all to come to repentance*" (2 Peter 3:9, emphasis added).

Jesus is patiently waiting for those future believers who will come to him. He is more patient than we realize but also more purposeful. Someone is going to be that "last believer" prior to the rapture, that final Christian in the church age who is part of a limited number of Gentiles chosen for salvation during the time of Israel's hardening. As Paul wrote to the Romans, "I do not want you, brethren, to be uninformed of this mystery—so that you will not be wise in your own estimation—*that a partial hardening has happened to Israel until the fullness of the Gentiles has come in*" (Romans 11:25, emphasis added).

When that last Gentile is saved, the trumpet will sound, and the Lord will descend. His patience during this age will have officially come to an end. The stage will now be completely set. The end-times players will be in their places. There will be no more previous prophecies to be fulfilled or background preparations to be made. The rapture will then happen in a flash, and then the lights will go out on planet Earth. The prophetic curtain of the biblical apocalypse will finally rise, revealing the Man of Sin and the tribulation's horrific hour of testing.

And history's final act will commence.

EIGHT

HORIZONS

Traveling by train within the United States, Bishop William Quayle was drawn into conversation with some of his fellow passengers. The bishop, who was not wearing his religious garb at the time, was asked by a curious passenger, "What is your line of business?" After a moment's reflection, the bishop replied, "Horizons!"

He was right. Everyone who believes and proclaims the gospel of the risen Christ and is waiting for his Second Coming travels and trades in "horizons."[1] End-time prophecy is all about horizons. The horizon is a distant, visible line or boundary separating heaven from earth. Just as a horizon serves as a clear dividing line between land and sky, the coming of Christ separates this age from the age to come, the present from the future, and the signs from the substance.

As we gaze at the horizon of our world today, storm clouds are gathering and darkening. That is what this book is all about.

All signs indicate that we are late in the day, and that the darkness of the end of days is quickly approaching.

> We face an apocalypse. The specter of death and economic collapse spread by the COVID-19 pandemic, the convulsive mass protests over police brutality coalescing with multiple preexisting crises: such things as global warming, identity crisis, fraying social fabric, polarized politics, tribalism, mass discontent, failing states, and an unraveling of global order. If we picture these crises together, the silhouettes of the four horsemen of the Apocalypse practically become visible on the horizon, primed to romp into our postmodern and post-Christian consciousness. Propelled as we were by seemingly limitless scientific-technological innovations, we thought we had left these four horsemen far behind, way back in the pre-modern world.
>
> We were wrong.[2]

That is a massive understatement. Signs all around us are lighting up like runway lights as the coming of Christ approaches. Recent polling reveals that most American evangelicals sense that the rapture and the commencement of the end times are just over the horizon. The Religion News Service reports that according to a recent poll, "41% of all U.S. adults, 54% of Protestants and 77% of Evangelicals believe the world is now living in the biblical end times."[3] Polls have uncovered the following:

> 58 percent of Americans think that another world war is "definite or probabl[e]."

41 percent "believe Jesus Christ will return" by the
  year 2050.

59 percent "believe the prophecies in the Book of
  Revelation will come to pass."[4]

Other polls have revealed a similar sentiment:

"55 percent of Americans believe 'that before the world
  ends the religiously faithful will be saved.'"

46 percent of Americans believe "the world will end in
  the Battle of Armageddon between Jesus and the
  Antichrist."[5]

Further, "research conducted by the Brookings Institute's
Center for Middle East Policy on Americans' attitudes toward
the Middle East and Israel found that 79 percent of Evangelicals
say they believe 'that the unfolding violence across the Middle
East is a sign that the end times are nearer.'"[6] "One in five believes
the world will end in their lifetime."[7]

These statistics clearly reveal a pervasive, collective sense,
especially among evangelicals, that the present and the horizon
are rapidly merging, becoming almost indistinguishable. Even
the most casual observer of our times senses that developments
in our world today strikingly foreshadow what lies ahead—just
over the horizon. Future events are casting their shadows before
them and are converging and accelerating as each day passes. In
this book so far, we examined in detail a major mile marker on
the pathway to the prophetic horizon—the emerging global system of control that will be instituted by the Antichrist in the end

times. As we have seen, this sign is significant and surging, but it is far from isolated. Additional prophetic harbingers are multiplying. Each of these signs is individually noteworthy, but viewed in aggregate, they dramatically point toward the end of the age.

Let's look briefly at five of these signs that point toward the coming of Jesus Christ and the wrapping up of this present age—five signs that all relate in one way or another to the great reset.

ISRAEL AND THE DEEPENING MIDDLE EAST CRISIS

In 2020, with the world still in the death throes of COVID-19, the Middle East was the lone global bright spot. Things in the world's most persistent flashpoint were looking up. Hope was in the air. The world was shocked and surprised as Arab nations lined up one after another to sign normalization of relations treaties with their once-hated nemesis Israel. The seventy-year stalemate was ended. This chain of agreements is known as the "Abraham Accords." In their wake, a new Middle East was heralded.

The Israel–United Arab Emirates agreement was the first domino to fall, with the announcement of an agreement on August 13, 2020. This was quickly followed by the Bahrain announcement on September 11. These agreements marked the first normalization of relations between an Arab country and Israel since Egypt in 1979 and Jordan in 1994. "The bilateral agreements formalize the normalization of Israel's already thawing relations with the United Arab Emirates and Bahrain in line with their common opposition to Iran."[8]

At the signing ceremony between Israel and United Arab Emirates and Bahrain on September 15, 2020, President Donald

Trump, speaking from a balcony overlooking the south lawn of the White House, said, "We're here this afternoon to change the course of history. After decades of division and conflict, we mark the dawn of a new Middle East."[9] And "Israeli Prime Minister Benjamin Netanyahu said the day 'is a pivot of history. It heralds a new dawn of peace.'"[10] Emirati foreign minister Sheikh Abdullah bin Zayed Al Nahyan said, "Today, we are already witnessing a change in the heart of the Middle East—a change that will send hope around the world."[11] Morocco followed suit in December 2020, followed by Sudan in January 2021.

Within a few months of those historic agreements, all illusions of lasting peace in the Middle East were punctured when Hamas indiscriminately fired more than four thousand rockets into Israel in May 2021, bringing the two parties to the brink of an all-out war. Israel unleashed a furious response, pounding Hamas's rocket positions and collapsing underground tunnels. As usual, the global outcry against Israel was deafening. Israel was smeared as an oppressor, and anti-Semitism around the world peaked. After eleven days of nonstop conflict, a truce was negotiated. Open hostilities ceased. But everyone knows it is just a brief break. The situation will continue to simmer until it boils over again at some point. The buildup is always brewing. Rockets will again dot the sky, Israel's Iron Dome defense system will shoot 90 percent of them out of the sky, and the entire bloody scene will be repeated until another temporary truce is brokered—or maybe not. Next time, or anytime, it could quickly spiral out of control into a regional firestorm. Prophetic flashpoints abound.

All of this is highly significant for end-time prophecy. It is no accident. First, the fact that Israel even exists as a modern nation is a miracle. The gathering of the Jewish people to their ancient homeland and the forming of the nation in 1948 has been accurately called the "Miracle on the Mediterranean." After 1,900 years of dispersion to more than seventy nations, and the death of the Hebrew language, a nation was reborn. No event since the first century is more prophetically significant. Israel's existence is the beginning point and necessary precondition for all end-time biblical prophecy. May 1948 was the watershed for prophetic fulfillment.

Second, the Bible says Israel will be a ceaseless source of frustration and irritation for the nations of the world. So much so, that in the end times the nations will tire of Israel's very existence and conspire to wipe the Jewish state off the map. Anti-Semitism will reach a global tipping point.

> Behold, I am going to make Jerusalem a cup that causes reeling to all the peoples around; and when the siege is against Jerusalem, it will also be against Judah. It will come about in that day that I will make Jerusalem a heavy stone for all the peoples; all who lift it will be severely injured. And all the nations of the earth will be gathered against it. (Zechariah 12:2–3)

Anti-Semitism is on the rise. Anti-Semitic attacks in the United States hit an all-time high in 2019.[12]

> Violence and harassment targeting American Jews broke out coast-to-coast amid the 11 days of fighting between Israelis and Palestinians that ended in a ceasefire on 20 May.
> Incidents included outdoor diners in Los Angeles who

were physically attacked by a group carrying Palestinian flags, violence against orthodox Jews in New York City—home to the largest population of Jews outside of Israel—and Nazi imagery posted on a synagogue in Alaska this week.

Pro-Palestinian protests and anti-Jewish vandalism at synagogues—which are quickly stepping up security due to the attacks—have also been documented in Illinois and Florida.[13]

In protest against Israeli policies, Ben & Jerry's stopped selling their products in the part of Israel known as the West Bank.[14] The United Nations continues to single out Israel for regular condemnation while overlooking repressive regimes. The United Nations General Assembly (UNGA) condemned Israel far more than any other nation in 2020. The total number of resolutions against Israel was seventeen compared with six for the rest of the world.[15]

What we see today should sadden us, but it should not surprise us. Israel will be a "heavy stone" for the nations until Jesus returns to earth.

Third, the event that commences the coming seven-year time of global tribulation is the signing of a peace agreement between the Antichrist and Israel (Daniel 9:27). The Abraham Accords, while not the fulfillment of this prophecy, are precursors to it. The enduring and escalating conflict between Hamas and Hezbollah on one side and Israel on the other side shows no signs of diminishing. Sadly, the opposite is true. Iran is arming and aiding its surrogates that surround Israel and egging them on to keep ratcheting up the pressure. Israel moves one step closer to all-out war as each day passes. Israel's only hope, from the human standpoint, is a comprehensive, guaranteed peace with the sea of enemies that surrounds its borders.

Enter the Antichrist. After the rapture of the church to heaven, Satan's masterpiece will rise, and his initial splash on the global scene will be brokering a peace agreement for Israel—the Abraham Accords on steroids. He will be heralded and applauded as the great peacemaker. Events in the Middle East today are ready for his entrance on the world stage. We can only imagine how the ensuing chaos after the rapture will intensify the state of affairs, providing the final impetus for the Antichrist's rise and his move into the Middle East maelstrom.

GLOBALISM

In a sense, this entire book is an exposé of globalism, so you might be wondering why we are taking time to consider globalism as a separate sign. That is a legitimate question. We will not spend much time discussing it further, but it is important to put the advance toward globalism in its broader biblical context.

In the early chapters of the book of Genesis, after the global flood, the entire world was gathered in one place with one purpose, under the rule of one godless leader, a man named Nimrod (Genesis 10–11). God had commanded humanity to spread out and take dominion over the earth, but shaking its collective fist in God's face, the global community settled down in Babel, constructing a city and creating a false religious system epitomized by the infamous Tower of Babel. In response to the rebellion, God confounded the language of humanity, scattering Babel's inhabitants and putting an abrupt end to the first global community.

Since that time, Satan has worked tirelessly to get the world back together again under the rule of one man. He will not settle for anything less than total global control. Through the millennia, the world has inexorably progressed from tribalism to nationalism back to globalism. Satan, the master globalist, is orchestrating events and manipulating world leaders to get the world back to Babel so he can control it all through one man. Fittingly, two of the final chapters in Revelation, chapters 17 and 18, prophesy the final destruction of the new Babylon in the end times, which will be the great political, economic hub of the world under the Antichrist's rule. History will come full circle. Satan will achieve his goal, albeit short-lived, of ruling the world under the control of a new Nimrod, the Antichrist.

The demonic drive toward globalism is an unmistakable sign of the times.

RUSSIA, IRAN, AFGHANISTAN, AND THE GOG INVASION

Over 2,500 years ago, the Jewish prophet Ezekiel foretold a massive invasion of the regathered people of Israel by a vast, aggressive coalition of nations led by a man identified as "Gog" who rises from the land of Magog (southern Russia and area in former Soviet republics).

The heart of the prophecy is found in Ezekiel:

> The word of the LORD came to me saying, "Son of man, set your face toward Gog of the land of Magog, the prince of Rosh, Meshech and Tubal, and prophesy against him and say, 'Thus

says the Lord GOD, "Behold, I am against you, O Gog, prince of Rosh, Meshech and Tubal. I will turn you about and put hooks into your jaws, and I will bring you out, and all your army, horses and horsemen, all of them splendidly attired, a great company with buckler and shield, all of them wielding swords; Persia, Ethiopia and Put with them, all of them with shield and helmet; Gomer with all its troops; Beth-togarmah from the remote parts of the north with all its troops—many peoples with you.

"Be prepared, and prepare yourself, you and all your companies that are assembled about you, and be a guard for them. After many days you will be summoned; in the latter years you will come into the land that is restored from the sword, whose inhabitants have been gathered from many nations to the mountains of Israel which had been a continual waste; but its people were brought out from the nations, and they are living securely, all of them. You will go up, you will come like a storm; you will be like a cloud covering the land, you and all your troops, and many peoples with you." (Ezekiel 38:1–9)

Three of the chief confederates in this coalition are Rosh, Persia, and Magog. Rosh has been identified as Russia, based on many linguistic, historical, and geographical connections.[16] Persia is the ancient name for the modern Islamic Republic of Iran. Afghanistan is part of ancient Magog.

In the last four decades, the emergence of Russia and Iran as two key global players has happened right on cue, and Afghanistan continues to fill the headlines. At the same time, Arab nations are pursuing détente with Israel, Iran is hell-bent on destruction, and Russia is a reliable, powerful Iranian ally to provide cover. Under the reign of its new czar, Vladimir Putin, Russia is poised to fulfill its role in the Gog prophecy as a close ally of Iran.

Iran's leaders harbor a hatred of Israel that is unmatched and unrivaled in today's world.

Iran's mullah regime is the world's largest sponsor of terrorism. Iran is the puppet master for a growing network of dangerous, loyal proxies. Rather than getting directly involved in Israel, Iran contracts its dirty work out to surrogates such as Hamas in Gaza (situated on Israel's southwest border) and Hezbollah in Lebanon (situated on Israel's northern border). Iran's shadow war with Israel could break out into open conflict at any time.

Below the surface of Iran's deep hatred for Israel is an apocalyptic ideology that is deeply ingrained in its mullahcracy. They view the United States as the "great Satan" and Israel as the "little Satan." Their stated goal is to rid the world of both nations. Their messianic ideology fuels this longing because they believe the Mahdi (Messiah) will make his final appearance in a time of warfare and bloodshed. They believe that sparking a confrontation with the United States and Israel will serve as a catalyst, putting out the "welcome mat" for the Mahdi and triggering the apocalypse. Iran's push to cross the nuclear finish line is upping the ante and could force Israel's hand to take military action to destroy or at least decelerate Iran's nuclear megaplex. Iran currently has enough nuclear fuel to arm one nuclear warhead.[17] In the coming months, if there is no change in circumstances, they will have enough to arm several more. They are also working on the ballistic missile technology to deliver the payload. A nuclear Iran is no longer a fear or threat; it is a jarring reality. Israel is making serious plans for an attack on Iran if the current trend cannot be reversed.[18]

Magog is also part of the end-time invasion of Israel. Ancient Magog is modern-day central Asia that includes all the Muslim nations that formed the underbelly of the former Soviet Union: Kazakhstan, Uzbekistan, Tajikistan, Turkmenistan, and Kyrgyz Republic. Another nation included in Magog is Afghanistan. The humiliating, ill-planned withdrawal of the United States from Afghanistan in 2021 left the Taliban in control of the country, along with remnants of Al-Qaeda and a shadowy group identified as ISIS-K. Whoever eventually comes out on top and seizes the levers of power in Afghanistan will certainly be a radical Islamic group. With all the weaponry left behind by the American military, the terrorists there will be well armed, and there is no doubt they will jump at the chance to join an alliance to wipe the Jewish state off the face of the earth.

Developing events in Afghanistan, in concert with the rise of Russia and Iran as allies, are another link in the chain of events leading to the fulfillment of the Gog-Magog war and hasten the countdown for the coming of Christ.

THE PLAGUE

COVID-19. Enough said. Everyone on the planet knows about this scourge that killed millions and shut down the global economy. Nothing since World War II has affected the world psyche and economy so dramatically. But many believe it also carries prophetic implications. McLaughlin & Associates polled likely US voters and found that "a stunning 44.3% of poll respondents said they believe the coronavirus and resulting economic meltdown is a 'wake up call for us to turn back to faith in God,' signs of 'coming judgment,' or both."[19] Furthermore, 29 percent of those polled believe the coronavirus crisis suggests that "we are living in what the Bible calls the 'last days.'"[20]

Jesus listed "pestilences" (diseases) as one of the "birth pains" that will portend his return to the earth (Matthew 24:8 NIV; Luke 21:11 NKJV). Many view COVID-19 as a direct fulfillment of those prophecies, but in the context of Luke 21:8, and the corresponding text in Matthew 24, Jesus was prophesying events that will unfold after believers are raptured to heaven and the time of tribulation begins. Three points bolster this view.

First, labor pains do not normally commence until shortly before the delivery of the baby. In the same way, the signs connected with the Lord's return will be condensed into a brief season just before he comes. Once they begin, they will accelerate and mushroom into an explosion of catastrophic events.[21]

Second, the imagery of birth pains consistently surfaces in Scripture in conjunction with the end times. Jeremiah said, "Ask and see: Can a man bear children? Then why do I see every strong man with his hands on his stomach like a woman in labor, every face turned deathly pale? How awful that day will be!" (Jeremiah 30:6–7 NIV). Likewise, the apostle Paul used the figure of birth pains in relation to cataclysms of the end times. "Now, brothers and sisters, about times and dates we do not need to write to you, for you know very well that the day of the Lord will come like a thief in the night. While people are saying, 'Peace and safety,' destruction will come on them suddenly, as labor pains on a pregnant woman, and they will not escape" (1 Thessalonians 5:1–3 NIV). Paul located birth pains in the final day of the Lord, another name for the tribulation.

A third reason to place the signs Jesus spoke of in the future time of tribulation is Jesus' repeated reference to "the end" (Matthew 24:6, 13, 14) and the reference to the "end of the age" in Matthew 24:3. These chronological markers point beyond this current era to the end of the age. Additionally, the time period Jesus spotlighted culminates with cosmic signs and his visible, glorious return to earth (Matthew 24:29–31).

Others have correlated coronavirus with the pale horse in Revelation 6:8 that unleashes four instruments of judgment: famine, war, pestilence, and the wild beasts of the earth. Again, the surrounding context, which mentions cosmic signs (Revelation 6:14–19), places these judgments in the future time of tribulation, not the current age. However, it is instructive that plagues in the end times are positioned right next to the "wild beasts of the earth" in Revelation 6:8. The majority of novel viruses that have emerged in the last thirty years, and infected humans, have originated with animals such as bats, monkeys, pigs, and birds. These zoonotic diseases are spilling over to humans at an alarming rate.

COVID-19 is not the direct fulfillment of Luke 21:11 or Revelation 6:8. Having said that, the coronavirus is a tiny window—a faint foreshadowing—of what lies ahead. It is a precursor to the death and devastation that will come from pestilence arising from the animal kingdom. It is also a pale preview of the paralyzing fear that will sweep the globe. As Rev. Mike Taylor recounted:

This new era, this new decade is clearly an epoch moment in history. I can remember as a young child in the 1950s getting under my desk at school. We would have air raid drills to practice getting ready in the event that Russia would attack us with a nuclear bomb. I remember the riots, Vietnam War, protests and the Cold War with Russia in the 1960s. I can recall the Middle East Wars, drug addiction, AIDS and many other diseases of the '70s, '80s and '90s. I have been through 9/11, terrorism and the great recession.

However, even after all I have been through and experienced over the last almost 70 years, I don't remember anything that compares to the coronavirus scare.[22]

Many people share that sentiment. Even with vaccines readily available and mandated, almost two-thirds of those who have received the vaccination are still apprehensive about life returning to normal.[23] Lingering fear still stalks the streets.

Jesus warned of worldwide panic in the end times: "People will faint from terror, apprehensive of what is coming on the world" (Luke 21:26 NIV). The sudden outbreak of coronavirus and the crippling fear it induced illustrate how ripe the world is for the jarring labor contractions of deadly diseases that will span the globe. As John MacArthur notes,

> That doesn't mean the era we are living in is the one Christ describes. But it *does* underscore the imminency of Christ's return for the church. The world in which we live is already ripe for the Tribulation. Elements like the birth-pang signs are already being felt. The present afflictions may merely be like Braxton-Hicks contractions—premature labor pains—but they nonetheless signify that the time for hard labor, and then delivery, is inevitable and quickly drawing near.[24]

That is an illuminating parallel. COVID-19 is not part of the birth pains Jesus forecasted but represents premature labor pains, signaling what is coming in the future tribulation.

As we also discussed at length in this book, the COVID-19 "plague" also serves as part of the global stage setting for the world government and commercial empire predicted in Revelation 13. Simply stated, COVID-19 is a hive for all kinds of effects and outcomes that extend far beyond the pandemic. The response by many government leaders has led some to aptly describe it as tyranny masquerading as safety. In that sense, it serves as another signpost on the road to Armageddon.

SOCIAL UNREST

Jesus said the end times will be characterized by swelling lawlessness and social disorder and a chilling of human affection. "Because lawlessness is increased, most people's love will grow cold" (Matthew 24:12). In the New Testament, this current age, the time span between the two comings of Christ, is the last days (Hebrews 1:2). The apostle Paul said that this broad time frame known as the last days will be punctuated by especially dangerous, perilous times:

> But realize this, that in the last days difficult times will come. For men will be lovers of self, lovers of money, boastful, arrogant, revilers, disobedient to parents, ungrateful, unholy, unloving, irreconcilable, malicious gossips, without self-control, brutal, haters of good, treacherous, reckless, conceited, lovers of pleasure rather than lovers of God. (2 Timothy 3:1–4)

The Greek word *chalepos* translated as "difficult" is found only one other place in the New Testament, Matthew 8:28, where it describes the wild, uncontrollable demoniacs. The word carries the idea of wild, violent, and savage. We are living today in one of the outbreaks of perilous, savage times. Chaos and turmoil are engulfing the world in flames. Cultural, societal, and racial upheaval rips at the heart of America and the world. Humanity is locked in a state of seething rage ready to explode at the slightest provocation. Our world is ablaze with violence, threats, and rage—on social media, on television news, on the highways, on the streets, in the halls of government, in schools, and even in homes.

Murder rates in major US cities are skyrocketing, turning them into urban "killing fields." The wave of unrest and violence has all kinds of societal implications, but prophetically it points toward the need for a forceful governmental response—a strong hand—to curb the unrest and restore law, order, and a reasonable modicum of safety. There is a growing wave in many places to "defund police," and that sentiment may find quarter in many places for a period of time, but eventually global law enforcement will become more draconian and heavy-handed than at any point in history. Revolt and rebellion will meet with heavy resistance. The Antichrist will control the world.

SCANNING THE HORIZON

During one of his encounters with the religious leaders of his day, Jesus sternly rebuked them for their blindness to the signs of the times of his first coming:

> The Pharisees and Sadducees came up, and testing Jesus, they
> asked Him to show them a sign from heaven. But He replied

to them, "When it is evening, you say, 'It will be fair weather, for the sky is red.' And in the morning, 'There will be a storm today, for the sky is red and threatening.' Do you know how to discern the appearance of the sky, but cannot discern the signs of the times?" (Matthew 16:1–3)

Jesus emerged from Galilee, seemingly out of nowhere, performing astounding miracles, signs, and wonders. The miracles Jesus performed were the very signs the Jewish prophets had announced would identify the Messiah. Yet the Jewish leaders were blind to the clear signs of his arrival. They totally missed the signs of the times—the signs that the Messiah was in their midst.

In the same way, many today are following their bad example. They are blind to the signs that are proliferating all around us—signs on the horizon—events related to God's program for the end of days. End-time prophecy is about horizons. Events that once seemed far off now appear to be right upon us. The world is moving inexorably toward a prophetic horizon predicted long ago in God's Word—a horizon of global control by the Antichrist. Global events are linking and fusing to bring that horizon into clearer focus. The Antichrist's horizon of horror is startlingly near.

But that horizon will eventually be swallowed up by the final horizon of global rule and reign when Jesus returns to earth to set up his worldwide kingdom. That is the real reset all of history is headed toward.

That reset is humanity's only hope.

It is your only hope, and our only hope.

NINE

THE FINAL RESET

For all the justified criticism that has been leveled against the great reset, there is one point the great resetters have right. There is one point we can all agree on. This world desperately needs a great reset. We need more than a simple tune-up. We need a total transformation.

Our planet is groaning and heaving. War, social and racial unrest, shattered families, surging suicide, runaway debt, inflation, deadly new viruses, drug and alcohol abuse, rising lawlessness, and political polarization are coalescing to drive civilization to its knees. In today's environment, good news can be difficult to find. Hope is in short supply. Our world is increasingly weary, worried, and worn. Something has to change. Something big. We all know it. We all know deep down inside that this world is not what it is supposed to be. We all yearn for things to be much better. We imagine utopia on earth—a new world order—a great society permeated with peace and prosperity, where everything is made right. But how in the world could that ever come to pass?

Is it even remotely possible? If so, who can possibly pull it off? Is there any hope?

One point should be clear by now. This final, ultimate reset we need for planet Earth will not come as a result of human effort, no matter how heroic. Humanity has created the mess, and humanity cannot fix the mess, as hard as we might try. It just keeps getting worse. The reset will not be produced by climate change advocates, the WEF, the Democrat Party, the Republican Party, peaceful protests, economic equality, the US government, the Chinese government, better laws, world religions, nuclear disarmament, or peace treaties.

The only true Global Resetter is God. Only the Creator can be the Re-Creator. Only the One who set the world in motion can reset it back to its original condition. God is the "Great Resetter," and the work of total transformation will commence on the day when he sends Jesus Christ, the Prince of Peace, back to planet Earth just as he promised two thousand years ago when Jesus ascended back to heaven. When Jesus fulfills that promise and comes back to earth, everything will change. His return to planet Earth is the fulcrum of history. All hope for this dying, broken, disintegrating world flows from the reality that he is coming again to conquer and receive the inheritance that Adam and Eve forfeited in the garden. He will do it.

In 47 BC at the Battle of Zela, the Roman army under Julius Caesar soundly defeated the forces of King Pharnaces, who fought the Romans for control of Pontus in Asia Minor. After his victory, Caesar returned to Rome and made his famous announcement, "*Veni, vidi, vici.*" "I came, I saw, I conquered."

Some seventeen hundred years later, a Polish military strategist, King John III Sobieski, led a brilliant campaign to drive the Ottoman invaders out of central Europe. Leading a force of twenty-five thousand men, he came to the aid of the German emperor Leopold I and beat the invaders back to the walls of Vienna, saving the city and the emperor. The Polish king was given audience before Pope Innocent XI, who congratulated him on his victory. King John's reply was classic: "I came, I saw, God conquered."

So shall it be in the last days. God will destroy the evil forces of hell and the wicked armies of the earth at the triumphal return of Jesus. Jesus will come, the world will see, and God will conquer. That will be the glorious consummation of history and the climax of this age.

But let's not get ahead of ourselves. Before Jesus comes to initiate the final, great global reset, there will be a great tribulation—a time worse than any period in history up to that point. Jesus spelled it out. "For then there will be a great tribulation, such as has not occurred since the beginning of the world until now, nor ever will" (Matthew 24:21). A great tribulation will precede global transformation. Things on this earth are going to get worse, much worse, before they get better. All the destabilizing forces we see at work in our world today will multiply and intensify and peak in the earth's final days.

Let's briefly survey where planet Earth is headed.

THE STORM BEFORE THE CALM

As we saw in chapter 7, someday, any day, the rapture of the church will occur. The rapture is the next event on God's prophetic calendar. Millions of people all over the globe will vanish into thin air in the time it takes to blink your eye. The rapture is God's prophetic trigger that will set the end times in motion.

In the wake of the rapture, a shocked, reeling world will scramble to find its footing and pick up the pieces. Out of the chaos, according to the prophet Daniel, a group of ten leaders, which we might call the G-10, will rise in a reunited Roman Empire, probably centered in Europe (Daniel 7:7–8). The G-10 will institute and oversee a return to some degree of order and calm and will elect a political strongman as head of their alliance. He will usher in a brief time of global peace and safety (Revelation 6:1–2). But the peace will be short-lived, as the world will plunge headlong into a time of global darkness Scripture calls the day of the Lord or tribulation (Matthew 24:9, 21; 1 Thessalonians 5:2–3).

The divine purpose of the tribulation is to punish the nations for their hardened, age-long rebellion against God, to purge and prepare Israel for its role in Messiah's kingdom, and to purchase an innumerable host of people who will turn to Jesus as their Savior during earth's darkest days (Revelation 7:9–17). God will use both the rapture and the tribulation as powerful evangelistic tools to bring people to himself for salvation. Even in the darkest times, our loving God will still seek and save those who are lost.

During the time of tribulation that will last seven years, a series of divine judgments will be poured on the world in scorching succession. These judgments are likened to birth pains several times in Scripture (Jeremiah 30:4–7; Matthew 24:8; 1 Thessalonians 5:3). As the tribulation progresses, like birth pangs, these judgments will intensify in both their severity and frequency. These three waves of God's judgment are described in detail in Revelation 6–19.

Seven Seal Judgments

First Seal (6:1–2)	White Horse: The Antichrist
Second Seal (6:3–4)	Red Horse: War
Third Seal (6:5–6)	Black Horse: Famine
Fourth Seal (6:7–8)	Ashen, or Pale, Horse: Death and Hades (Hell)
Fifth Seal (6:9–11)	Martyrs in Heaven
Sixth Seal (6:12–17)	Universal Upheaval and Devastation
Seventh Seal (8:1–2)	The Seven Trumpets

Seven Trumpet Judgments

First Trumpet (8:7)	Bloody Hail and Fire: One-Third of Vegetation Destroyed
Second Trumpet (8:8–9)	Fireball from Heaven: One-Third of Oceans Polluted
Third Trumpet (8:10–11)	Falling Star: One-Third of Fresh Water Polluted
Fourth Trumpet (8:12)	Darkness: One-Third of Sun, Moon, and Stars Darkened
Fifth Trumpet (9:1–12)	Demonic Invasion: Torment[1]
Sixth Trumpet (9:13–21)	Demonic Army: One-Third of Mankind Killed
Seventh Trumpet (11:15–19)	The Kingdom: The Announcement of Christ's Reign

Seven Bowl Judgments

First Bowl (16:2)	Upon the Earth: Sores on the Worshipers of the Antichrist
Second Bowl (16:3)	Upon the Seas: Water Turned to Blood, All Marine Life Dies
Third Bowl (16:4–7)	Upon the Fresh Water: Turned to Blood
Fourth Bowl (16:8–9)	Upon the Sun: Intense, Scorching Heat
Fifth Bowl (16:10–11)	Upon the Antichrist's Kingdom: Darkness and Pain
Sixth Bowl (16:12–16)	Upon the River Euphrates: Dried Up; Armageddon
Seventh Bowl (16:17–21)	Upon the Air: Earthquakes and Hail

As you can see, the efforts of the great resetters can never lead to utopia. All their godless, humanistic, satanically energized efforts will only plunge the world into death and dystopia. Utopia on earth apart from God is impossible. As the famous preacher Charles Spurgeon once said, "Apart from the second Advent of our Lord, the world is more likely to sink into a pandemonium than to rise into a millennium."[2]

After the bowls are poured out, God will take care of one final order of business, as Babylon, which is the Antichrist's global headquarters and the world's political-commercial center, is destroyed forever (Revelation 17–18). Babylon, the original epicenter of human rebellion in Genesis, will meet its final doom, as the biblical story winds to a close and comes full circle.

At the end of the seven-year period of hell on earth, with the world on the verge of total destruction, Jesus Christ will physically, visibly, gloriously return to earth. He will return as conquering King to receive his inheritance promised by the Father (Psalm 2:8). No event in Scripture is described so gloriously and graphically. Here are just a few of the classic Second Coming texts.

> For I will gather all the nations against Jerusalem to battle. . . .
> Then the LORD will go forth and fight against those nations,
> as when He fights on a day of battle. In that day His feet will
> stand on the Mount of Olives, which is in front of Jerusalem
> on the east; and the Mount of Olives will be split in its middle
> from east to west by a very large valley. (Zechariah 14:2–4)

> But immediately after the tribulation of those days the sun
> will be darkened, and the moon will not give its light, and the
> stars will fall from the sky, and the powers of the heavens will

be shaken. And then the sign of the Son of Man will appear in the sky, and then all the tribes of the earth will mourn, and they will see the Son of Man coming on the clouds of the sky with power and great glory. (Matthew 24:29–30)

But when the Son of Man comes in His glory, and all the angels with Him, then He will sit on His glorious throne. (Matthew 25:31)

And I saw heaven opened, and behold, a white horse, and He who sat on it is called Faithful and True, and in righteousness He judges and wages war. His eyes are a flame of fire, and on His head are many diadems; and He has a name written on Him which no one knows except Himself. He is clothed with a robe dipped in blood, and His name is called The Word of God. (Revelation 19:11–13)

George Eldon Ladd said it well: "Here is a simple but profound biblical truth which cannot be overemphasized: apart from the person and redeeming work of Jesus Christ, history is an enigma. . . . Christ, and Christ alone, has the key to the meaning of human history. . . . Apart from the victorious return of Christ, history is going nowhere."[3]

As you can imagine, Christ's return will spark a fast-moving sequence of stunning events. First, Jesus will decimate the gathered armies of the Antichrist in the land of Israel at Armageddon and throughout the land and will seize the Antichrist and his henchman, the false prophet, and cast them alive into the lake of fire (Revelation 19:20–21).

Second, not everyone on the earth will be slain at Armageddon.

People will still be living all over the earth, clinging to survival as the earth's ecology nears total destruction. Jesus will gather all those still living on earth for judgment (Matthew 25:31–46).

Third, at the same time, Old Testament saints and believers who were martyred during the tribulation will be resurrected, reviewed, and rewarded (Daniel 12:1–3; Revelation 20:4–6).

Fourth, Satan will be bound by a strong angel and cast in the abyss, where he will be imprisoned for one thousand years (Revelation 20:1–3).

Fifth, a huge temple, the fourth Jewish temple, will be constructed in Jerusalem as the hub of global worship during the earthly reign of Christ (Ezekiel 40–44).

According to Daniel 12, all of this, and many other events, will transpire during a seventy-five-day period immediately following Jesus' return to Earth. The seventy-five-day period after Christ's return to Earth will be like the time between the election of a US president in November and the inauguration in January. Preparations for the new administration are set in place. Agendas are established. Appointments are made. Arrangements are set in order. In the same way, everything will be prepared for the beginning of the reign of Christ.

THE MILLENNIUM

When all the setup is in place, the global reign of Jesus, the goal of all human history, will be inaugurated—the reign of the Messiah over the earth—a period of time known as the millennium. The word *millennium* comes from two Latin words that, when combined, mean "one thousand years." The words "thousand years" are repeated six times in Revelation 20:1–7. The millennium is the one-thousand-year period when Satan is bound and Christ reigns on the earth with his redeemed people. It is Satan's chain and the Savior's reign. The millennium will be phase one of God's eternal kingdom—the front porch of eternity.

The Bible has a lot more to say about the coming millennium than most people realize.

Professor and Bible teacher Dwight Pentecost said, "A larger body of prophetic Scripture is devoted to the study of the millennium, developing its character and conditions, than any other one subject."[4] Dozens of Old Testament texts give major details about the nature and conditions of the messianic kingdom. Following are a few of the prominent features of the millennium:

1. **Permanent Peace**—There will be no more wars, rumors of wars, or conflicts. Jesus will rule the nations as benevolent King. The one-thousand-year reign of Jesus could be called the *Pax* Messiah (messianic peace) (Isaiah 2:4; 9:4–7; 11:6–9; Zechariah 9:10).
2. **Perpetual Happiness**—A spirit of exuberant joy and happiness will fill the earth. Depression and discouragement will disappear (Isaiah 9:3–4; 12:3–6; 14:7–8; 25:8–9; 30:29; 42:1; Jeremiah 30:18–19; Zephaniah 3:14–17; Zechariah 10:6–7).
3. **Pervasive Glory**—The whole earth will be engulfed in God's glory (Isaiah 35:2; 40:5; 60:1–9; Ezekiel 43:1–5).
4. **Prevailing Justice**—When the millennial kingdom begins, it will be inhabited only by believers. Those who survive the tribulation period will still have their physical human bodies with a fallen nature. Those who were raptured

or resurrected will have glorified bodies and perfected spirits. Believers in their human bodies will have children who will also possess mortal flesh. Any outbreak of sin or rebellion will be judged by the administration of perfect justice by the Messiah (Isaiah 9:7; 11:5; 32:16; 42:1–4; 65:21–23). He will rule the nations with "a rod of iron" (Revelation 2:27), restraining and reproving sin so that the prevailing environment in the kingdom will be righteousness and justice (Isaiah 11:1–5; 60:21; Jeremiah 31:23; Ezekiel 37:23–24; Zephaniah 3:1, 13). The human yearning for a just society will finally be realized.

5. **Perfect Health Care**—The millennial health-care plan will be out of this world. There will not be any PPOs, Medicare, Medicaid, physicians, or hospitals. Jesus will take care of bodies as well as souls (Isaiah 29:18; 33:24; 35:5–6; 61:1–2; Ezekiel 34:16). Those living on the earth in human bodies during the millennium will live long life spans as in the days before the flood (Isaiah 65:20).

6. **Profound Prosperity**—Hunger, thirst, and homelessness will not exist. We will not need stockbrokers, IRAs, bank accounts, investment advisers, or Wall Street. No inflation, recession, or depression will disrupt or drag down the global economy. Prosperity will thrive under the wise leadership of King Jesus (Isaiah 35:1–2, 7; Ezekiel 34:26; 36:29–30; Amos 9:13–14; Micah 4:1, 4).

We could go on and on, but you get the idea. The millennium will be the utopia and paradise humans have always written about, dreamed about, and imagined, only infinitely better.

Chuck Swindoll describes the millennial reign of Christ:

The book of Revelation promises a golden age in which all weapons of warfare will be fashioned into implements of peace. Prosperity will be shared. Peace will become the banner of all people. The light of justice will illumine every corner of the world. This condition will not be achieved through educational funding, political change, social programs, cultural awakening, or even religious revival. . . . True global transformation will occur only when Satan and his minions are ousted, allowing Jesus Christ and His glorified saints to rule over the earth.[5]

Jesus will not rule alone. Believers living in glorified bodies will reign with Christ during the millennium in positions of authority based on the degree of our faithfulness during our earthly lives. Someone once described our present lives as "training time for reigning time." The life you live today will determine your life in eternity. When Jesus comes, he will review and reward your faithfulness and give you a kingdom assignment. Therefore, we need to carefully and wisely invest what he has given us to maximize the return.

THE END

When the one thousand years has run its resplendent course, Satan will be released from the abyss and will lead a brief, final rebellion that will be quickly put down by Jesus. This final conflict is called the war of Gog and Magog (Revelation 20:7–10). Satan's second coming will prove that even after one thousand years locked in the abyss, Satan will be the same. His nature will remain unchanged. As a result, Satan, the global antagonist, and his demonic army, will be cast into the lake of fire forever. The devil, who made his entrance on the world stage in Genesis 3:1, will exit the global stage forever.

Satan's final sentence will be followed by the final judgment of all lost humans, who refused to trust God's gracious provision for salvation and forgiveness. In one of the Bible's most sobering scenes, those who appear at the great white throne will be condemned to the lake of fire (Revelation 20:11–15).

With all judgment finalized, this present universe will be destroyed in a fiery conflagration of cosmic proportions. The apostle Peter described the "uncreation" of the universe:

> But the day of the Lord will come like a thief, in which the heavens will pass away with a roar and the elements will be destroyed with intense heat, and the earth and its works will be burned up. Since all these things are to be destroyed in this way, what sort of people ought you to be in holy conduct and godliness, looking for and hastening the coming of the day of God, because of which the heavens will be destroyed by burning, and the elements will melt with intense heat! But according to His promise we are looking for new heavens and a new earth, in which righteousness dwells. (2 Peter 3:10–13)

After this act of uncreation, God will create a new heaven and new earth. The heavenly city, the new Jerusalem, will come down out of heaven to sit on the new earth, serving as a capital for the new creation (Revelation 21:1–2). This city, the size of a floating continent (a 1,400-mile cube), is also known as the third heaven. It is the abode of God where his throne sits, the Tree of Life grows, the streets are paved with gold, the gates are massive pearls, and the glory of God shines and illuminates the entire creation. It will be a complete reversal or reset of the original creation.

Paradise Lost (Gen. 1–2)	Paradise Regained (Rev. 21–22)
Heavens and earth created	New heaven and earth
Sun created	No more sun
Night established	No night
Seas created	No sea
Curse announced	No more curse
Death enters history	No more death
Man driven from the tree	Man restored to paradise
Sorrow and pain begin	No more tears or pain

If you are running low on hope these days, set aside time often to think about the world to come. Take time to read Revelation 20–22, develop an eternal perspective, and seek to live a righteous life in view of what lies ahead.

Above all else, make sure you will be part of the new world. Do not miss what life is all about—a relationship with the living God through his Son, Jesus Christ. He will re-create your life and give you a great reset if you will call out to him and trust him for your eternal salvation. That reset will secure your place in the future reign of Christ in the re-creation.

FROM RAPTURE TO RE-CREATION

- The rapture occurs suddenly in a moment of time (1 Corinthians 15:51–58; 1 Thessalonians 4:13–18).
- After an unknown amount of time of further preparation and stage setting, the tribulation officially begins when the Antichrist forges a seven-year treaty with Israel (Daniel 9:27).
- During the first half of the tribulation, the Antichrist gains power, the seal judgments are opened, and the 144,000 Jewish witnesses begin their ministry (Revelation 7:1–8).
- The second half of the tribulation is dominated by the global reign of the Antichrist and institution of his mark. Also, the trumpet and bowl judgments will be unleashed.
- At the end of the tribulation, the campaign of Armageddon occurs (Revelation 16:16).
- Christ returns to the Mount of Olives and slays the armies gathered against him throughout the land, from Megiddo to Petra, south of the Dead Sea (Isaiah 34:1–6; 63:1–5; Revelation 19:11–16).
- Interval or transition period of seventy-five days passes (Daniel 12:12):
  - › The Antichrist and the False Prophet are cast in the lake of fire (Revelation 19:20–21).
  - › Tribulation survivors (both Jews and Gentiles) are regathered, reviewed, and rewarded (Matthew 25).
  - › Old Testament and tribulation saints are resurrected (Daniel 12:1–3; Isaiah 26:19; Revelation 20:4).
  - › Satan is bound in the abyss (Revelation 20:1–3).

- Christ reigns on the earth for one thousand years (Revelation 20:4–6).
- Satan's final revolt and defeat occur (Revelation 20:7–10).
- The great white throne judgment takes place (Revelation 20:11–15).
- The present heavens and earth are destroyed (Matthew 24:35; 2 Peter 3:3–12; Revelation 21:1).
- The new heavens and new earth are created (2 Peter 3:13; Revelation 21:1).
- Eternity (Revelation 21:9–22:5).

TEN

RESETTING YOUR LIFE

A great global reset is coming. That much is sure. All things will ultimately be made new by God himself. There is no greater hope for God's people than that. We are eagerly looking for the end times. But what about the meantime? How do we live in the meantime as we await Christ's coming and the end times? How can we effectively navigate the reset before the reset?

This book has demonstrated that the agenda of the WEF and global elites is advancing, and as it accelerates, believers in Jesus Christ will find ourselves increasingly in the crosshairs. Even now, believers are vilified and viewed as the main opposition to progress. We are in the way of their agenda. So how do faithful believers live today in a culture that is increasingly hostile to us and our beliefs? How can we adjust and reset our personal lives to maximize our impact for Christ and glorify God?

There is a great story about two brothers who got into a fight with each other. Hearing the commotion from a distance, the mother of the two boys rushed to break up the scuffle and find out what was going on. After scolding both of them, the mother asked, "Who started it? Who delivered the first blow?" The younger brother spoke up and said, "I hit him before he hit me." Now that is a young man who was not going to allow himself to be surprised. He anticipated what was coming and was ready for it. In the same way, Christians need to anticipate persecution and mistreatment at the hands of a lost world.[1] We need to anticipate the blows of the enemy and not be surprised when they hit us.

The New Testament instructs us again and again to expect opposition and persecution for what we believe. Jesus said, "Blessed are you when people insult you and persecute you, and falsely say all kinds of evil against you because of Me" (Matthew 5:11). "If the world hates you, keep in mind that it hated me first. If you belonged to the world, it would love you as its own. As it is, you do not belong to the world, but I have chosen you out of the world. That is why the world hates you" (John 15:18–19 NIV). The apostle Paul, who himself had persecuted believers, wrote, "For it has been granted to you on behalf of Christ not only to believe in him, but also to suffer for him" (Philippians 1:29 NIV). "In fact, everyone who wants to live a godly life in Christ Jesus will be persecuted" (2 Timothy 3:12 NIV).

The apostle Peter echoed the same sentiment in his first epistle. He said plainly not to be surprised when the world persecutes you (1 Peter 4:12). Few admonitions are more relevant to our current situation. For believers in Jesus Christ, persecution comes with the territory. It is par for the course. We should expect it. After all, our leader, our Savior, was crucified. He was rejected by this world. If we look anything like Jesus, this world will hate us too. If we love God and his truth and morality, the world will hate us. The symbol of Christianity is a cross. We should not be surprised at suffering and rejection. It should not catch us off guard. After all, we are the Master's minority. Believers have been hunted, hounded, and harassed throughout church history.

Yet, it is easy for those of us living in the West to be caught off guard by the cost of following Christ. As Erwin Lutzer said, "The Christian poet Vasily Zhukovsky wrote, 'We all have crosses to bear, and we are constantly trying on different ones for a good fit. We are all trying to find a lighter cross.'"[2] In doing that, we forget our calling and forget that in many places today Christians are being led like lambs to the slaughter. The World Evangelical Alliance reports:

> Over 200 million Christians in at least 60 countries are denied fundamental human rights solely because of their faith.
>
> It is estimate[d] that approximately 176,000 Christians were martyred from mid-2008 to mid-2009.
>
> If current trends continue, it is estimated that by 2025, an average of 210,000 Christians will be martyred annually.[3]

The majority of governmental religious restrictions are aimed at Christians. "Some international humanitarian agencies have estimated that 80% of all religious persecution in the world today is aimed at Christians."[4] Sadly, that is the world we live in, and if the global resetters establish their agenda, the vice grip of persecution against followers of Christ will increase.

By God's providence and mercy, America has largely been sheltered and shielded from religious persecution, but that is rapidly changing. A colossal cultural shift is underway. The winds of change are blowing. An epic cultural reset is sweeping our country. There is a spiritual climate shift, or what we might call "spiritual climate change." Hostility against Christians is surging. We no longer enjoy a home-field advantage. Erwin Lutzer said,

> In the past, we, as American Christians, always had home-field advantage. We knew that in the crowd there were those from the other team who were opposed to us, but the larger stadium crowd was either on our side or indifferent to our witness as Christians. All that has changed. Now we play our games on enemy turf. A minority is on our side while the wider culture sits in the stands shouting hateful epithets at us, rejoicing in our losses. And the elitists in the skyboxes cheer them on.[5]

More and more we find ourselves swimming against the tide. Preaching the gospel and practicing the morality of our faith puts us on a collision course with our culture. As Philip De Courcy said:

> The Christian who preaches the exclusivity of the Gospel of Jesus Christ is labeled a bigot; the Christian who opposes gay marriage is called homophobic; the Christian who questions the transgender agenda is called hateful; the Christian who espouses the biblical record of Creation is pegged as anti-intellectual; and the Christian who questions the growth of governmental power is considered antisocial. The list goes on, but the point is simple. Winds of social and ethical change are blowing across America, and they are blowing into the faces of Bible-believing Christians.[6]

Increasingly in our culture, biblical Christians are the piñatas, the punching bags, of society. Christians are quickly becoming cultural outsiders, being pushed to the margins. It is open season to mock, malign, scorn, and denigrate believers in Jesus Christ.

So, what do we do? How do we respond? Do we give up and throw in the towel? Do we collapse in despair and retreat from the broader culture? Do we resort to anger and hostility, meeting the world on its own level? What do we do in a society that is increasingly hostile to Christ and Christians?

First Peter provides a timeless template for a personal and corporate reset in light of increasing opposition to our faith:

> Beloved, do not be surprised at the fiery ordeal among you, which comes upon you for your testing, as though some strange thing were happening to you; but to the degree that you share the sufferings of Christ, keep on rejoicing, so that at the revelation of His glory you may rejoice with exultation. If you are reviled for the name of Christ, you are blessed, because the Spirit of glory and of God rests on you. Make sure that none of you suffers as a murderer, or thief, or evildoer, or a troublesome meddler; but if anyone suffers as a Christian, he is not to be ashamed, but is to glorify God in this name. For it is time for judgment to begin with the household of God; and if it begins with us first, what will be the outcome for those who do not obey the gospel of God? AND IF IT IS WITH DIFFI-CULTY THAT THE RIGHTEOUS IS SAVED, WHAT WILL BECOME OF THE GODLESS MAN AND THE SINNER? Therefore, those also who suffer according to the will of God shall entrust their souls to a faithful Creator in doing what is right. (4:12–19)

This passage highlights four things we need to in times like these to reset our lives spiritually.

REALISM

The apostle Peter penned his first epistle to groups of believers scattered in five Roman provinces located in ancient Asia Minor, which is modern-day Turkey. He probably wrote to them not long before the fires of Nero's persecution burned in Rome in AD 64. Although the Neronian persecution was limited to the city of Rome and its immediate environs, if that persecution had already occurred when Peter wrote, it would be strange for him not to mention it. The immediate crisis for Peter's original audience was an escalation of mistreatment by the surrounding culture in the form of insults, slander, and reviling (1 Peter 1:6; 3:9; 4:14). The mistreatment was verbal and social, not physical. The persecution also was not state sponsored or systematic. It was local, sporadic persecution. We might call it "soft persecution" or "low-grade persecution."

As you can see, there is a striking parallel between the addresses in 1 Peter in the first century and believers in the twenty-first century. Aligning with Christ puts believers today at odds with the prevailing culture. It makes us a target of the world. We feel the slings and arrows of this world. We are singled out in the public square as objects of scorn and derision. We come under sustained enemy fire. The persecution, at least up to this point, is almost exclusively verbal and social, just as it was with Peter's audience. It takes the form of mockery, maligning, social media bans, and sometimes exclusion from employment opportunities. Businesses are punished for refusing to participate in events that violate their conscience. Students in school cannot mention God. Evangelical leaders are excluded from government functions and events for taking biblical stands on clear moral issues. Pro-family Christian ministries are labeled as "domestic hate groups." These are not isolated events, and the rhetoric is steadily being ratcheted up. So far the persecution is verbal and social, but it could quickly escalate to harder forms of mistreatment, just as it often did in the early church and in later church history.

Peter alerted his original readers, and us, that in the midst of mocking and mistreatment, we need a good dose of realism. We are not to be shocked or surprised when we suffer for the sake of the gospel. We are not to think of it as a strange thing. We should expect it. "Just as soldiers expect death, athletes expect pain, students expect homework, and mothers expect exhaustion, so Christians should expect the world's hostility and hatred."[7]

Peter called what his readers were enduring a "fiery ordeal." Some believe this refers to believers literally being burned alive as martyrs. However, as stated previously, there is no evidence in 1 Peter or secular history from that time that this was happening in Roman provinces in Asia. The words "fiery ordeal" are metaphorical. Nevertheless, they spotlight the severity of the suffering. Christians were social outcasts who were ridiculed and discriminated against simply because they were Christians, but Peter said this should not surprise us.

The difficulty we face here in America is that we have had it so good for so long that persecution takes us by surprise. It has happened so suddenly that Christians in America are saying or at least thinking, "I can't believe our country is doing this—that this is actually happening in America." But we'd better believe it. It is reality. Peter reminded us not to think it's strange and not to be surprised. First Peter 4:12 should set our expectations, saving us from disappointment and disillusionment.

Persecution seeks to marginalize believers by eliminating or diminishing our voice—to put the squeeze on us to shut us up, to silence us while the work of the global resetters moves forward unopposed or at least with as little resistance as possible. Peter reminds us that this should not surprise us. He said you should not be surprised that the world that hates him hates you. If you live like Jesus, look like him, and preach his gospel, you will suffer like him. The world seems to like and admire Jesus. However, the Jesus the world today admires is not the Jesus of the Bible. The Jesus who tolerates evil, whitewashes sin, never speaks a harsh word, and never sends anyone to hell is a fictional figment of their imagination. When we present the real Jesus, shine his light, and expose the darkness, we will face an inevitable backlash. When we call sin "sin," and tell people Jesus is the only way to God, the world will not like it.

Of course, God has a higher purpose in all of this than just persecution. Concerning our mistreatment by the world, Peter said it "comes upon you for your testing" (1 Peter 4:12). God allows us to suffer to refine our faith. His sovereign purpose is not to destroy us but to develop us. God allows us to undergo the crucible of suffering not to disprove our faith but to prove it. There is purpose in our pain. There is design in our difficulty. God does not waste our suffering. We are purified and purged like gold in a furnace as we suffer. The world seeks to ruin us, but God uses their mistreatment to refine us and transform us into his image.

So, our first response when under the gun from society is to *adjust our expectations.*

REJOICING

Our second response is to *adjust our emotions.* In the midst of mistreatment, Peter not only encouraged realism but also encouraged rejoicing. When opposition comes, we are not called merely to endure it but to exult in it. Obviously, we do not enjoy suffering. We do not rejoice that we suffer. But we do rejoice that we can suffer for Christ's sake. Matthew 5:11–12 tells us that suffering for Christ's sake is a blessing, not a curse. Philippians 1:29 says that suffering for Christ is a gift. "For it has been granted to you on behalf of Christ not only to believe in him, but also to suffer for him" (NIV). We should count it a privilege to suffer for the One who suffered for us.

To help us with this, Peter gave two key reasons we can rejoice in the midst of mistreatment.

The Prospect

Very simply, Peter reminded us that present suffering will be followed by future glory. This is one of the key themes in 1 Peter. We suffer now, but glory is coming. The cross leads to the crown. Peter said, "To the degree that you share the sufferings of Christ, keep on rejoicing, so that also at the revelation of His glory you may rejoice with exultation" (1 Peter 4:13).

We must look beyond temporary, present suffering to life everlasting. There is future glory and present blessing. We find this same truth expressed elsewhere in Scripture:

In this you greatly rejoice, even though now for a little while, if necessary, you have been distressed by various trials. (1 Peter 1:6)

For I consider that the sufferings of this present time are not worthy to be compared with the glory that is to be revealed to us. (Romans 8:18)

On July 4, 1952, at the age of thirty-four, Florence Chadwick waded into the water off the coast of Catalina Island, hoping to be the first woman to swim the twenty-one-mile strait to California. The fog was thick, so thick she could not even see the boats in her own party. The water was numbingly frigid. In spite of the conditions, Chadwick swam on for fifteen hours, but finally, numbed by the cold, she asked to be taken from the water. Almost immediately after entering the boat she realized she was within a half mile of the shore. She lamented giving up, saying, "If only I would have been able to see the shore, I could have made it."

Filled with renewed confidence, two years later, in similar weather conditions, Chadwick successfully swam the strait. She said the reason for her success was, "I always kept the image of the shore in my mind."[8]

When we get discouraged about the conditions around us and the opposition we face, let's resolve to keep the eternal shoreline ever before us. Our eventual success is assured. The crown awaits us. The road marked with righteous suffering is the road that leads to glory. We can rejoice in suffering because of future glory, but the second reason we can rejoice in suffering is that there is present blessing.

The Presence

During times of mistreatment, we are promised the presence of God in a unique, heightened sense. As we faithfully suffer for his sake, God draws near to us, administers his strength, and provides an extra measure of his abiding presence. First Peter 4:14 says, "If you are reviled for the name of Christ, you are blessed, because the Spirit of glory and of God rests on you." The words "if you are reviled" form a conditional clause that assumes the truth of the statement. We could translate it "since you are being insulted." In other words, that was the present experience of Peter's readers. Peter said that during those times the Lord draws near to us in a unique way. This was the experience of Daniel's three friends in the fiery furnace (Daniel 3:24–25), Stephen at his stoning (Acts 7:56), and Paul as he faced his trial in Rome with no human support (2 Timothy 4:17).

John G. Paton was a missionary to New Hebrides among vicious cannibals. He faced many harrowing situations and close calls with death. On one occasion, he fled for his life and spent an entire night hiding in a chestnut tree as angry cannibals frantically searched for him below. He related his experience of that night in the tree:

> I climbed into the tree, and was left there alone in the bush. The hours I spent there live all before me as if it were but of yesterday. I heard the frequent discharge of muskets, and the yells of the Savages. Yet I sat there among the branches, as safe in the arms of Jesus. Never, in all my sorrows, did my Lord draw nearer to me, and speak more soothingly to my soul, than when the moonlight flickered among these chestnut leaves, and the night air played on my throbbing brow,

as I told all my heart to Jesus. Alone, yet not alone! If it be to glorify my God, I will not grudge to spend many nights alone in such a tree, to feel again my Savior's spiritual presence, to enjoy His consoling fellowship.[9]

What comforting words as we face those who revile us: "Alone, yet not alone."

Of course, the Lord will never leave or forsake any believer. We are never alone. But when we faithfully stand for him in times of mistreatment for his name, he promises to be with us in an intensified sense. In those times, we enjoy a heightened awareness of his presence and peace.

For these two reasons, we can rejoice even in our mistreatment. We experience his presence now and the prospect of his coming in the future. We enjoy present blessing and future glory.

REEVALUATION

In 1 Peter 4:15–18, the apostle Peter added an important caveat or qualification to Christian suffering:

If you suffer, it should not be as a murderer or thief or any other kind of criminal, or even as a meddler. However, if you suffer as a Christian, do not be ashamed, but praise God that you bear that name. For it is time for judgment to begin with God's household; and if it begins with us, what will the outcome be for those who do not obey the gospel of God? And, "If it is hard for the righteous to be saved, what will become of the ungodly and the sinner?" (NIV)

Simply stated, if you bring persecution on yourself, you should be ashamed and embarrassed. You should expect to suffer for your own folly and disobedience. If you commit sin, you are merely reaping the consequences of the wrongdoing you have sown. You deserve what you are getting. Make sure you do not suffer for your own faults and foolishness. Peter then listed a few serious sins the believer should not be associated with: "murderer or thief or any other kind of criminal, or even as a meddler." We all know about murder, stealing, and other kinds of crimes, but what does it mean to be a "troublesome meddler"? This seems to be out of place with such a serious list of crimes.

The Greek word translated "troublesome meddler" appears only here in the New Testament. In this context, it means more than just being nosy or a busybody. It carries the idea of badgering and baiting people who do not conform to Christian standards. It refers to someone we might call an "agitator" who stirs things up and gets in someone's face. In context, it denotes unwise interfering and excessive zeal in attacking and opposing unbelievers. As we confront a culture that is at best unfriendly and at worst outwardly hostile, avoid unnecessarily pouring fuel on the fire. Many believers are deeply upset at the degradation and downward spiral of America, and rightfully so. Believers are not the majority anymore (if we ever were), but let's not become an angry, vindictive minority. Do not be an angry, agitated Christian. In our world today, we need less anger and more anguish. Make sure it is the gospel that offends people, not you. Needlessly agitating unbelievers leads to greater hostility and hardening. Baiting and badgering people who do not conform to Christian standards is not pleasing to God, even though it may make us feel better temporarily. That does not mean we have to shrink back and be cowards. We must be courageous in perilous times. We must stand boldly and uncompromisingly for the gospel. But we must also be prudent. We must be proportionate. We must be careful not to roll up culture wars issues and politics with the gospel.

There is a story about a man who went to visit his pastor about his wife's uncontrollable, explosive anger. He told the pastor that when he arrived home every evening, his wife would often yell and scream at him and even throw things. He was at a loss to know what to do. He asked the pastor if he would mind coming home with him to see it for himself so he could counsel him effectively. The pastor reluctantly agreed. When the two men arrived at the front door of the house and were about to go in, the man turned to the pastor and said, "Please wait here while I go in and get her started." Let's make sure we are not like that husband. Let's make sure we do not start it. Let's make sure we do not unnecessarily incite the world's ire by our unwise meddling and agitation.

Peter referred to those who suffer as "Christian." This is significant because this word appears only three times in the New Testament (Acts 11:26; 26:28). The word *Christian* means "those of Christ's party," "a Christ one," or "belonging to Christ." The term was originally used by enemies of Christianity as a term of reproach and insult to believers. It was a slur, yet followers of Jesus owned it and wore it as a badge of honor.

The gist of 1 Peter 4:17–18 is that what believers suffer now cannot be compared with what is in store for unbelievers later. It is an argument from the lesser to the greater or what Jews often called from light to heavy. As I once heard someone say, "If you have to choose between a smooth flight with a crash landing and a bumpy flight with a safe landing, opt for the bumpy flight." If this present suffering and mistreatment are hard for those of us who are being saved, imagine what judgment will be like for the unsaved when Christ comes in judgment. It is an encouragement for us to endure suffering faithfully and is, at the same time, a sober warning for the lost.

RELIANCE

The fourth and final key to launching a personal reset in an increasingly hostile culture is reliance on the Lord. "Therefore, those also who suffer according to the will of God shall entrust their souls to a faithful Creator in doing what is right" (1 Peter 4:19). The Greek word translated by the English word *entrust* is a banking term. The word means to deposit for safekeeping. That means we are to give our souls into the safekeeping of God. Jesus is our example of this kind of total reliance as he died unjustly on the cross. He said, "Father, INTO YOUR HANDS I COMMIT MY SPIRIT" (Luke 23:46). Speaking of Jesus' brutal mistreatment, 1 Peter 2:23 says, "While being reviled, He did not revile in return; while suffering, He uttered no threats, but kept entrusting Himself to Him who judges righteously."

Likewise, when we experience mistreatment from the culture, we must deposit ourselves into God's safekeeping, trusting that our deposit will yield eternal dividends. Peter referred to God as the "Creator." This is the only time in the New Testament the noun *Creator* is used of God. Peter refers to God as Creator to highlight God's ability to care for us no matter what happens. As Creator, he gives and governs life. He rules in complete, comprehensive sovereignty. The Lord we trust is the architect of the ages. He feeds the birds and beasts. He numbers the hairs of our heads. He will watch over us who commit ourselves to his care, so we must trust him. There is an old saying, "You can't talk about standing on the Rock of Ages and then act as if you're clinging to your last piece of driftwood." What a terrible testimony for us to claim to trust in our faithful Creator and yet fail to rely on him when the heat is turned up. We must maintain faith in the faithfulness of God who can be fully trusted for our todays and our tomorrows. In a world of shifting tides and gathering storms, it is a great blessing to anchor our hope in a faithful, sovereign Creator. We cling to One who is immovable and immutable when everything that has been nailed down is being ripped up. Entrust your soul to him, entrust your life to him, and entrust your future to him.

Entrusting yourself to the Lord begins by entrusting your heart and soul to him for the first time by trusting in Jesus as your Savior from sin. If you have never personally accepted Jesus Christ as your Savior from sin and entrusted your eternity to him, then you need to accept him right now. The only way to come into a relationship with God and gain admission to heaven is through God's Son, Jesus Christ. You must admit you are a sinner, acknowledge that you cannot save yourself, and accept Jesus as the Savior you need. You must personally receive him by faith. You must accept Christ and what he has done for you. "But as many as received Him [Jesus], to them He gave the right to become children of God" (John 1:12). When you receive Christ, God promises to give you the precious gift of eternal life. "He who believes in the Son has eternal life" (John 3:36).

If you have never trusted Jesus as your Savior, why not stop right now and call upon the Lord, accepting Christ as your personal Savior? Do it now. Do not put it off. There is no doubt that it is thrilling to know the future of the world—to know what will happen to this planet. That is primarily what this book is all about. Yet, as electrifying as that is, it is infinitely more exciting and comforting to know your future—to know what will happen to you when your life ends or when Jesus comes, whichever happens first. There is nothing better than knowing that your eternal soul has been committed forever to God for safekeeping.

Our sincerest prayer is that everyone who reads this book will be ready when Jesus comes. That you will experience the ultimate, eternal reset that comes through faith in Jesus Christ.

NOTES

Chapter 1: Global PRE-Set

1. "Our Mission," World Economic Forum, accessed July 14, 2021, https://www.weforum.org/.
2. Christopher Alessi, "Who' s Coming to Davos 2020, and Everything Else You Need to Know," World Economic Forum, January 17, 2020, https://www.weforum.org/agenda/2020/01 /davos-2020-who-is-coming-and-everything-you-need-to-know/.
3. Klaus Schwab, "Now Is the Time for a 'Great Reset,'" World Economic Forum, June 3, 2020, https://www.weforum.org /agenda/2020/06/now-is-the-time-for-a-great-reset/.
4. Lora Ries and Mark Morgan, "The Biden Border Crisis," Heritage Foundation, January 31, 2022, https://www.heritage .org/biden-border-crisis.
5. "World Economic Forum Annual Meeting," World Economic Forum, accessed July 14, 2021, https://www.weforum.org/events /world-economic-forum-annual-meeting-2020.
6. Klaus Schwab, "What Is Stakeholder Capitalism?" World Economic Forum, January 22 2021, https://www.weforum .org/agenda/2021/01/klaus-schwab-on-what-is-stakeholder -capitalism-history-relevance/.
7. Sarita Nayyar, "Why It's Time to Start Talking About Consumption Equality," World Economic Forum, February 14,

2020, https://www.weforum.org/agenda/2020/02/consumption -equality-wealth-equality-fair-society/.

8. Alan Reynolds, "How One Model Simulated 2.2 Million U.S. Deaths from COVID-19," *CATO at Liberty* (blog), April 21, 2020, https://www.cato.org/blog/how-one-model-simulated-22-million -us-deaths-covid-19.

9. Natasha Anderson and Nexstar Media Wire, "New CDC Report Shows 94% of COVID-19 Deaths in US Had Contributing Conditions," WFLA News Channel 8, August 30, 2020, https:// www.wfla.com/community/health/coronavirus/new-cdc-report -shows-94-of-covid-19-deaths-in-us-had-underlying-medical -conditions/.

10. Jeffrey A. Tucker, "Lockdown Suicide Data Reveal Predictable Tragedy," American Institute for Economic Research, May 22, 2020, https://www.aier.org/article/lockdown-suicide-data-reveal -predictable-tragedy/.

11. Klaus Schwab and Thierry Malleret, *COVID-19: The Great Reset* (Geneva: Forum, 2020), 4.

12. Schwab and Malleret, 19.

13. Schwab and Malleret, 22.

14. John Mecklin, "This Is Your COVID Wake-Up Call: It Is 100 Seconds to Midnight," *Bulletin of the Atomic Scientists*, January 27, 2021, https://thebulletin.org/doomsday-clock /current-time/.

15. Schwab and Malleret, *COVID-19*, 114.

16. Schwab and Malleret, 160.

17. Schwab and Malleret, 161.

18. Schwab and Malleret, 168.

19. Yuval Noah Harari, "The World After Coronavirus," *Financial Times*, March 20, 2020, https://www.ft.com/content/19d90308 -6858-11ea-a3c9-1fe6fedcca75.

20. Schwab and Malleret, *COVID-19*, 243–44.

21. Peter Bakker and John Elkington, "To Build Back Better, We Must Reinvent Capitalism. Here's How," World Economic

Forum, July 13, 2020, https://www.weforum.org/agenda/2020/07/to-build-back-better-we-must-reinvent-capitalism-heres-how/.

22. According to the CDC's website, their definition of an actual vaccine is as follows: "Vaccine: A product that stimulates a person's immune system to produce immunity to a specific disease, *protecting the person from that disease.*" By all accounts involving "breakthrough cases," none of the COVID-19 vaccines have fully accomplished this. CDC Healthy Schools, "Immunization: The Basics," reviewed June 28, 2019, https://www.cdc.gov/healthyschools/bam/diseases/vaccine-basics.htm.

23. "CDC Recommends Pediatric COVID-19 Vaccine for Children 5 to 11 Years," Centers for Disease Control and Prevention, November 2, 2021, https://www.cdc.gov/media/releases/2021/s1102-PediatricCOVID-19Vaccine.html.

24. Daniel Estrin, "Highly Vaccinated Israel Is Seeing a Dramatic Surge in New Covid Cases. Here's Why," NPR, August 20, 2021, https://www.npr.org/sections/goatsandsoda/2021/08/20/1029628471/highly-vaccinated-israel-is-seeing-a-dramatic-surge-in-new-covid-cases-heres-why.

25. "About Parliament: Treaty of Rome (EEC)," European Parliament, Europa.eu, accessed July 15, 2021, https://www.europarl.europa.eu/about-parliament/en/in-the-past/the-parliament-and-the-treaties/treaty-of-rome.

Chapter 2: Surging Global Delusion

1. Deyan G., "How Much Time Does the Average American Spend on Their Phone in 2021?" techjury, updated December 7, 2021, https://techjury.net/blog/how-much-time-does-the-average-american-spend-on-their-phone/.

2. David Roach, "Bible Reading Drops During Social Distancing," *Christianity Today*, July 22, 2020, https://www.christianitytoday.com/news/2020/july/state-of-bible-reading-coronavirus-barna-abs.html.

3. See also Luke 22:53; Acts 26:18; Ephesians 6:12; Colossians 1:13.

4. Sarah Mae Saliong, "DC Talk's Kevin Max Announces He's an 'Exvangelical' Who Believes in the 'Universal Christ' After 'Deconstructing', 'Progressing,'" *Christianity Today*, May 19, 2021, http://www.christianitydaily.com/articles/11915/20210519 /dc-talk-s-kevin-max-announces-he-s-an-exvangelical-who -believes-in-the-universal-christ-after-deconstructing -progressing.htm.

5. Those who worship the Beast include only people whose names have "not been written before the foundation of the world in the book of life of the Lamb who was slain" (Revelation 13:8 ESV).

6. William Hendriksen, *New Testament Commentary: Thessalonians, Titus, Timothy* (Grand Rapids, MI: Baker, 1955), 184.

7. D. Edmond Hiebert, *The Thessalonians Epistles: A Call to Readiness* (Chicago, IL: Moody, 1971), 317.

Chapter 3: One World Under the Antichrist

1. We know the angels had already been created before the earth and humans were (Job 38:4–7). The temptation of Eve took place in Genesis 3:1–7, sometime after day seven of creation. Therefore, it is possible Satan's sin and expulsion from heaven took place shortly after day seven.

2. Ancient Jewish historians maintain that Nimrod built the tower in direct defiance against God, lest he try to flood the earth again. He wanted a tower so high the floodwaters of divine wrath would be unable to reach them.

    Flavius Josephus, *Antiquities of the Jews*, bk. 1, in *Josephus: The Complete Works*, chap. 4, accessed July 16, 2021, https:// www.ccel.org/ccel/josephus/complete.ii.ii.iv.html.

3. *El Elyôn* is Hebrew for "Most High God."

4. H. D. Northrop, *Beautiful Gems of Thought and Sentiment* (Boston, MA: Colins-Patten, 1890), 248.

5. Mecklin, "This Is Your COVID Wake-Up Call" (see chap. 1, n. 14).

6. "Rocket & Mortar Attacks Against Israel by Date," Jewish Virtual Library, accessed July 16, 2021, https://www.jewishvirtuallibrary. org/palestinian-rocket-and-mortar-attacks-against-israel.

7. The context of this chapter and its prophecies, beginning in verse 24, along with biblical history, make it clear that Daniel's "weeks" are periods of seven years. Therefore, "seventy weeks" corresponds to $70 \times 7 = 490$ years. The first 483 (seven weeks and sixty-two weeks) of those years are described as the time period from the "issuing of a decree to restore and rebuild Jerusalem until Messiah the Prince" (Daniel 9:25). Then, following the sixty-two weeks, "the Messiah will be cut off" (v. 26). This amazing prophecy was fulfilled to the day! This is followed by a "prophetic gap" between the sixty-ninth and seventieth weeks. That last week (of seven years) is the time described covering the Antichrist's treaty with Israel.

8. Maayan Jaffe-Hoffman, "Number of Jews in Israel and Worldwide on the Rise," *Jerusalem Post*, September 27, 2019, https://www.jpost.com/israel-news/number-of-jews-in-israel -and-worldwide-on-the-rise-reports-603033.

9. Nathan Jones wrote, "By placing the timing of the Gog-Magog Battle early in the Tribulation, the defeat and disillusionment of Muslims worldwide would destroy the strength of Islam. With the Church removed in a Pre-Tribulation Rapture, Christianity would also be removed. The resulting polytheistic and pantheistic religions would integrate well into the apostate one-world religion that the False Prophet promotes (Revelation 13:11–15). The only monotheistic religions left to reject the Antichrist would be Judaism and the newly growing Jesus movement, both of which the Antichrist persecutes greatly during the second half of the Tribulation (Revelation 6:11)." Nathan Jones, "Understanding Gog and Magog (Part 5 of 7)," *Christ in Prophecy Journal*, April 6, 2021, https:// christinprophecyblog.org/2021/04/understanding-gog-and -magog-part-5-of-7/.

10. Ezekiel 38 states that this invasion will take place in the "latter years" or "the last days" (vv. 8, 16), when Israel is "living securely" in the land (v. 14). It will also take place chronologically somewhere between the regathering of Israel (Ezekiel 37), which began on May 14, 1948, and Israel's spiritual rebirth, which occurs at the end of the tribulation, extending into the millennial kingdom (Ezekiel 40–48). So, under what circumstances might Israel be living securely? Obviously, in a post–Gog-Magog war era, Israel would be free from enemy threat, as all of Israel's worst enemies will have been annihilated in the war (Ezekiel 38:17–23). This would surely be a time of peace for Israel, further protected by the Antichrist's treaty.

Chapter 4: 666 and the Coming Cashless Society

1. "Shaping the Post-Crisis World," World Economic Forum, accessed January 19, 2022, https://widgets.weforum.org/history /2009.html.

2. Simon Hooper, "Davos Delegates Gather to 'Shape New World,'" CNN.com, January 27, 2009, https://edition.cnn.com/2009 /BUSINESS/01/27/davos.tuesday.crisis/index.html.

3. "Shaping the Post-Crisis World."

4. Elijah Mvundura, "The Collapse of Liberal Democracy," *Liberty*, November/December 2020, https://www.libertymagazine.org /article/the-collapse-of-liberal-democracy.

5. Erwin W. Lutzer, *We Will Not Be Silenced: Responding Courageously to Our Culture's Assault on Christianity* (Eugene, OR: Harvest House, 2020), 24.

6. James Corbett, "The Birth of the Cashless Society," *Hoboken 411*, September 15, 2020, https://hoboken411.com/archives/139428.

7. David Rosenthal, "The Global Rise of Authoritarianism and the Social Credit (Digital Surveillance) System," *Zion's Fire*, November–December 2020, 4, http://www.wordexplain.com /PDFdocs/David_Rosenthal_The_Rise_of_Global _Authoritarianism.pdf.

8. Mehul Desai, "The Benefits of a Cashless Society," World Economic Forum, January 7, 2020, https://www.weforum.org /agenda/2020/01/benefits-cashless-society-mobile-payments/.

9. James T. Areddy, "China Creates Its Own Digital Currency, a First for Major Economy," *Wall Street Journal*, April 5, 2021, https://www.wsj.com/articles/china-creates-its-own-digital-currency-a-first-for-major-economy-11617634118.

10. Areddy.

11. Corbett, "The Birth of the Cashless Society."

12. Desai, "The Benefits of a Cashless Society."

13. Desai.

14. David Solway, "The Great Reset and Klaus Schwab," *Jewish Voice*, December 5, 2020, https://thejewishvoice .com/2020/12/the-great-reset-and-klaus-schwab/.

15. Jeff John Roberts, "NFL Player 'Paid in Bitcoin' as Price Nears $30,000," *Fortune*, December 30, 2020, https://www.msn.com /en-us/money/markets/nfl-player-paid-in-bitcoin-as-price-nears -dollar30000/ar-BB1cm5gg.

16. Henry M. Morris, *The Revelation Record: A Scientific and Devotional Commentary on the Prophetic Book of the End of Times* (Wheaton, IL: Tyndale House, 1983), 252.

17. Arnold G. Fruchtenbaum, *The Footsteps of the Messiah*, rev. ed. (Tustin, CA: Ariel, 2003), 255.

18. Fruchtenbaum, 255.

19. John F. Walvoord, *The Prophecy Knowledge Handbook* (Wheaton, IL: Victor Books, 1990), 587.

20. M. R. De Haan, *Studies in Revelation* (Grand Rapids, MI: Zondervan, 1946; repr. Grand Rapids, MI: Kregel, 1998), 189. Citations refer to the Kregel edition.

21. Nicol Turner Lee, Samantha Lai, and Emily Skahill, "Vaccine Passports Underscore the Necessity of U.S. Privacy Legislation," Brookings, June 28, 2021, https://www.brookings.edu/blog /techtank/2021/06/28/vaccine-passports-underscore-the -necessity-of-u-s-privacy-legislation/.

22. Hugo Martín, "COVID Vaccine 'Passports' in the U.S.: Here's What We're Getting and Why," *Los Angeles Times*, June 14, 2021, https://www.latimes.com/business/story/2021-06-14/covid -vaccine-passport-united-states.

23. This list appears in Mark Hitchcock's book *The End* (Carol Stream, IL: Tyndale Momentum, 2012), 342–43.

Chapter 5: Enter the Dragon: China, the Reset, and the End of Days

1. Aya Velázquez, "China and the 'Great Reset,'" Medium.com, December 18, 2020, reposted Aya loves politics, November 28, 2020, https://ayavela.substack.com/p/coming-soon ?r=b5o2c&utm_campaign=post&utm_medium=web&utm _source=copy.

2. Hal Brands, "The Chinese Century?" *National Interest*, February 19, 2018, https://web.archive.org/web/20210314121311 /https://nationalinterest.org/feature/the-chinese-century-24557.

3. "China to Leapfrog U.S. as World's Biggest Economy by 2028— Think Tank," January 11, 2021, World Economic Forum, https:// www.weforum.org/agenda/2021/01/china-worlds-biggest -economy-usa-think-tank-covid-coronavirus/.

4. Eamon Barrett, "China Wants to Be a Leading Space Power by 2045—and It's Getting There Fast," *Fortune*, May 29, 2021, https://fortune.com/2021/05/30/china-space-race-rocket -landing-mars-us/.

5. Statista, "Number of Mobile Cell Phone Subscriptions in China from February 2020 to February 2021," April 2021, https://www .statista.com/statistics/278204/china-mobile-users-by-month/.

6. Velázquez, "China and the 'Great Reset.'"

7. Velázquez.

8. David Rosenthal, "The Global Rise of Authoritarianism and the Social Credit (Digital Surveillance) System," *Zion's Fire*, November–December 2020, 4.

9. Alexandra Ma and Katie Canales, "China's 'Social Credit' System Ranks Citizens and Punishes Them with Throttled Internet

Speeds and Flight Bans if the Communist Party Deems Them Untrustworthy," *Business Insider*, updated December 24, 2021, https://www.businessinsider.com/china-social-credit-system -punishments-and-rewards-explained-2018–4.

10. Ma and Canales.
11. James T. Areddy, "China Creates Its Own Digital Currency, a First for Major Economy," *Wall Street Journal*, April 5, 2021, https://www.wsj.com/articles/china-creates-its-own-digital -currency-a-first-for-major-economy-11617634118.
12. Ma and Canales, "China's 'Social Credit' System."
13. Rosenthal, "The Global Rise of Authoritarianism."
14. Michael Rectenwald, "The Great Reset, Part III: Capitalism with Chinese Characteristics," Mises Institute, January 1, 2021, https://mises.org/wire/great-reset-part-iii-capitalism-chinese -characteristics.
15. Rectenwald.
16. Rectenwald.
17. Grant R. Osborne, *Revelation*, Baker Exegetical Commentary on the New Testament, ed. Moises Silva (Grand Rapids, MI: Baker Academic, 2002), 381.

Chapter 6: America at Dusk

1. See Jeff Kinley, *The End of America?* (Eugene, OR: Harvest House, 2017), 137.
2. Stefan Zenker, "A Study of History—Arnold J. Toynbee," Stefan Zenker, last edited May 2, 2011, https://www.zenker.se/Books /toynbee.shtml.
3. Joella Straley, "It Took a Eugenicist to Come Up with 'Moron,'" *Code Switch* (NPR blog), February 10, 2014, https://www.npr.org /sections/codeswitch/2014/02/10/267561895/it-took-a-eugenicist -to-come-up-with-moron.
4. On many occasions, Pharaoh hardened his own heart (Exodus 7:13–14, 22; 8:15, 19, 32; 9:7, 34–35; 13:15). But on other occasions, God himself hardened Pharaoh's heart (Exodus 4:21; 7:3; 9:12;

10:1, 20, 27; 11:10; 14:4, 8, 17). In several of these instances, Pharaoh had hardened his own heart before God further hardened it.

5. David Jeremiah, *Is This the End? Signs of God's Providence in a Disturbing New World* (Nashville: W Publishing Group, 2016), 8.

6. Jeremiah, 9.

7. Charles Hodge, *Commentary on the Epistle to the Romans* (Grand Rapids, MI: Eerdmans, 1993), 42.

8. Franjo Gruber, Jasna Lipozenčić, and Tatjana Kehler, "History of Venereal Diseases from Antiquity to the Renaissance," *Acta Dermatovenerol Croatica* 23, no. 1 (2015): 1–11, https://pubmed .ncbi.nlm.nih.gov/25969906/.

9. Centers for Disease Control and Prevention, "Sexually Transmitted Diseases," *Gay and Bisexual Men's Health* (blog), last reviewed March 9, 2016, https://www.cdc.gov/msmhealth /STD.htm.

10. Gail Labovitz, "Feminist Sexual Ethics Project: Same-Sex Marriage," brandeis.edu, accessed July 23, 2021, https://www .brandeis.edu/projects/fse/judaism/docs/essays/same-sex -marriage.pdf, 1, 4.

11. Amy Carmichael, *Things As They Are: Mission Work in Southern India* (1905; n.p.: Pantianos Classics, 2016), 120.

Chapter 7: What Are We Waiting For?

1. "Rapture Party Day," Days of the Year, accessed July 23, 2021, https://www.daysoftheyear.com/days/rapture-party-day/.

2. Stephen Tompkins and Dan Graves, eds., "#101: The Didache," modernized and abridged from *The Teaching of the Disciples*, trans. J. B. Lightfoot, Christian History Institute, accessed July 23, 2021, https://christianhistoryinstitute.org/study/module /didache.

3. See the following (emphasis added):

Romans 13:11—"Knowing the *time*, that it is *already* the hour."

Romans 13:12—"The night is almost gone, and the day is *near*."

1 Corinthians 1:7—"*Awaiting eagerly* the revelation of our Lord Jesus Christ."

1 Corinthians 16:22—"*Maranatha*" (used by the early church for "hello" or "goodbye," from an Aramaic expression meaning "our Lord, come").

Philippians 3:20—"For our citizenship is in heaven, from which also we *eagerly wait* for a Savior."

Philippians 4:5—"The Lord is *near*."

1 Thessalonians 1:10—"To *wait* for His Son from heaven."

Titus 2:13—"*Looking for the blessed hope* and the *appearing* of the glory of our great God and Savior, Christ Jesus."

James 5:7–8—"Therefore be patient, brethren, until the *coming of the Lord* . . . be patient; strengthen your hearts, for the coming of the Lord is *near*."

Hebrews 9:28—"So Christ also . . . will *appear a second time* for salvation without reference to sin, *to those who eagerly await Him*."

Hebrews 10:25—"Encouraging one another; and all the more *as you see the day drawing near*."

Hebrews 10:37—"For yet *in a very little while*, He who is coming *will come*, and will *not delay*."

1 Peter 1:13—"*Fix your hope* completely on the grace to be brought to you at the revelation of Jesus Christ."

1 Peter 4:7—"The end of all things is *near*."

1 John 2:18—"We *know* that it is the *last hour*."

Jude v. 21—"*Waiting anxiously* for the mercy of our Lord Jesus Christ."

Revelation 3:11—"I *am coming quickly*; hold fast what you have."

Revelation 22:7—"Behold, *I am coming quickly*."

Revelation 22:12—Behold, *I am coming quickly*."

Revelation 22:20—"Yes, *I am coming quickly*."

4. Here are all the verses where *harpazo* is used in the New
   Testament, along with the meaning in each context:
   >Matthew 11:12—take by force
   >Matthew 12:29—carry off
   >Matthew 13:19—snatches away
   >John 6:15—take by force
   >John 10:12—snatch by force
   >John 10:29—snatch by force
   >Acts 8:39—snatch away, "disappear"
   >Acts 23:10—take away by force
   >2 Corinthians 12:2—caught up to heaven
   >2 Corinthians 12:4—caught up into Paradise
   >1 Thessalonians 4:17—caught up . . . in the clouds
   >Jude v. 23—(quickly) snatching out of the fire
   >Revelation 12:5—(referring to Jesus) caught up to God (at
   the ascension)
5. Though Jesus used the same Jewish wedding imagery in
   Matthew 25, he was referring to his second coming and Israel's
   readiness to receive her Messiah, not the rapture of the church.
6. Samuel Crossman, "Farewell, Vain World, I Must Be Gone,"
   Hymnary.org, https://hymnary.org/text/farewell_vain_world
   _i_must_be_gone.

Chapter 8: Horizons

1. "New Horizons," Know the Truth: The Teaching Ministry of
   Philip de Courcy, November 20, 2012, https://www.ktt.org
   /resources/truth-matters/new-horizons-0.
2. Mvundura, "The Collapse of Liberal Democracy," 4 (see chap. 4,
   n. 4).
3. Religion News LLC, "Shock Poll: Startling Numbers of
   Americans Believe World Now in the 'End Times,'" press release,
   September 11, 2013, http://religionnews.com/2013/09/11/shock
   -poll-startling-numbers-of-americans-believe-world-now-in-the
   -end-times/.

4. Jeff Brumley, "Global Events, Prophecy Stir Talk of 'End Time' Beliefs," *Florida Times-Union*, July 16, 2012, https://www.jacksonville.com/story/news/2010/07/17/global-events-prophecy-stir-talk-end-times-beliefs/15938318007/.

5. Douglas Todd, "We Need to Bring End-Times Beliefs Out of Their Closet," *Vancouver Sun*, November 8, 2008, https://www.pressreader.com/canada/vancouver-sun/20081108/282432754992615.

6. Walter Einenkel, "New Survey Shows That About 80% of Evangelicals Believe the 'End Times' Are Near," *Daily Kos*, December 7, 2015, http://www.dailykos.com/story/2015/12/7/1457887/-New-survey-shows-that-about-80-of-Evangelicals-believe-the-end-times-are-near.

7. Jeremy Weber, "Survey Surprise: Many Americans See Syria as Sign of Bible's End Times," *Christianity Today*, September 13, 2013, http://www.christianitytoday.com/gleanings/2013/september/syria-survey-end-times-armageddon-lifeway.html.

8. Deb Riechmann, Matthew Lee, and Jonathan Lemire, "Israel Signs Pacts with 2 Arab States: A 'New' Mideast?" AP, September 15, 2020, https://apnews.com/article/bahrain-israel-united-arab-emirates-middle-east-elections-7544b322a254ebea1693e387d83d9d8b.

9. Riechmann, Lee, and Lemire.

10. Riechmann, Lee, and Lemire.

11. Riechmann, Lee, and Lemire.

12. Max Matza, "Who's Behind Recent Rise in US Anti-Semitic Attacks?" BBC News, May 28, 2021, https://www.bbc.com/news/world-us-canada-57286341.

13. Matza.

14. Will Feuer, "Ben & Jerry's Board Chair Says 'I Am Not Anti-Semitic' After Sales Ban," *New York Post*, July 28, 2021, https://nypost.com/2021/07/28/ben-jerrys-board-chair-i-am-not-anti-semitic-after-sales-ban/.

15. "Israel Most Condemned by UN in 2020—Three Times Other

Nations," *Aljazeera*, December 24, 2020, https://www.aljazeera.com/news/2020/12/24/un-condemns-israel-most-in-2020-almost-three-times-rest-of-world.

16. Wilhelm Gesenius, *Complete Edition of Gesenius' Hebrew and Chaldee Lexicon* (Grand Rapids, MI: Eerdmans, 1949), 752; Clyde E. Billington Jr., "The Rosh People in History and Prophecy (Part Three)," *Michigan Theological Journal* 4 (1993); Clyde E. Billington Jr. "The Rosh People in History and Prophecy (Part Two)," *Michigan Theological Journal* 3 (1992); Jon Mark Ruthven, *The Prophecy That Is Shaping History* (Fairfax, VA: Xulon, 2003); James D. Price, "Rosh: An Ancient Land Known to Ezekiel," *Grace Theological Journal* 6 (1985).

17. "Iran Nuclear 'Breakout Time' Could Be Weeks If Not Restrained—Blinken," Reuters, June 7, 2021, https://www.reuters.com/world/middle-east/iranian-breakout-time-will-fall-weeks-if-not-constrained-blinken-2021–06–07/.

18. Alisa Odenheimer and David Wainer, "Israel Prepared to Attack in Iran, Defense Minister Says," Bloomberg, August 5, 2021, https://www.bloomberg.com/news/articles/2021-08-05/israel-is-prepared-to-attack-in-iran-defense-minister-says-kryq29zn; Anna Ahronheim and Tovah Lazaroff, "Gantz: Israel Is Ready to Strike Iran," *Jerusalem Post*, August 7, 2021, https://www.jpost.com/israel-news/israel-is-ready-to-strike-iran-gantz-675897.

19. Joel C. Rosenberg, "Coronavirus Pandemic Is a Wake Up Call: Exclusive Joshua Fund Poll," Joshua Fund, March 2020, https://www.joshuafund.com/learn/news-article/coronavirus_pandemic_is_a_wake_up_call_exclusive_joshua_fund_poll.

20. Paul Bedard, "Poll: 29% See Biblical 'Last Days,' 44% Say Virus Is God's 'Wake-Up Call,'" *Washington Examiner*, March 31, 2020, https://www.washingtonexaminer.com/washington-secrets/poll-29-see-biblical-last-days-44-say-virus-is-gods-wake-up-call.

21. John F. MacArthur Jr., *Matthew 24–28* (Chicago: Moody, 1989), 15.

22. Mike Taylor, "Taylor: During These Perilous Times, Faith in God

Wins over Fear," *Carroll County Times*, April 25, 2020, https://www.baltimoresun.com/maryland/carroll/lifestyles/cc-rl-taylor-042520-20200425-jgistm7tpnc4jgo6ulc54ctzzu-story.html.

23. Healthinsurance.com, "62% Have Apprehensions About Life 'Returning to Normal' Post COVID-19 Pandemic," PR Newswire, March 19, 2021, https://www.prnewswire.com/news-releases/62–have-apprehensions-about-life-returning-to-normal-post-covid-19–pandemic-301250735.html.

24. John F. MacArthur Jr., *The Second Coming* (Wheaton, IL: Crossway, 2006), 89.

Chapter 9: The Final Reset

1. The locusts in Revelation 9 are not literal. Their detailed description, including not eating plants and arising from the underworld, designates them as demonic beings.

2. Charles Spurgeon, "The Form of Godliness Without the Power" (sermon, Metropolitan Tabernacle, Newington, UK, June 2, 1889), Spurgeon's Sermons (vol. 35), https://www.ccel.org/ccel/spurgeon/sermons35.xxvii.html.

3. George Eldon Ladd, *A Commentary on the Revelation of John* (Grand Rapids, MI: Eerdmans, 1972), 82.

4. J. Dwight Pentecost, *Things to Come: A Biblical Study in Eschatology* (n.p.: Dunham, 1958; repr. Grand Rapids, MI: Zondervan, 2010), 476. Citations refer to the Zondervan edition.

5. Charles R. Swindoll, *Insights on Revelation* (Grand Rapids, MI: Zondervan, 2011), 258.

Chapter 10: Resetting Your Life

1. Philip De Courcy, *Take Cover: Finding Peace in God's Protection* (Washington, DC: Salem, 2018), 29.

2. Erwin W. Lutzer, *We Will Not Be Silenced* (Eugene, OR: Harvest House, 2020), 17.

3. Patrick O'loughlin, "News from the Front Lines," Sermon Central, September 19, 2011, https://www.sermoncentral.com

/sermons/news-from-the-front-lines-patrick-o-loughlin-sermon
-on-persecution-160569.

4. Gregory C. Cochran, *Christians in the Crosshairs* (Wooster, OH: Weaver, 2016), 23.

5. Lutzer, *We Will Not Be Silenced*, 17.

6. De Courcy, *Take Cover*, 31.

7. De Courcy, 33.

8. Erwin W. Lutzer, "Prayer That We Might Be Motivated to Live in Anticipation of the Lord's Return," Moody Church Media, December 15, 2013, https://www.moodymedia.org/blog/2013/01 /prayer-we-might-be-motivated-live-anticipation-lords-return/.

9. James Paton, *The Story of John G. Paton, Told for Young Folks: Or, Thirty Years Among South Sea Cannibals* (London, UK: Hodder & Stoughton, 1898), 175.

ABOUT THE AUTHORS

MARK HITCHCOCK has authored more than thirty books related to Bible prophecy, with total sales of over one million copies. He has appeared on MSNBC, Fox News, and hundreds of nationwide radio programs. He has earned ThM and PhD degrees from Dallas Theological Seminary and is an associate professor there. He lives in Edmond, Oklahoma, with his wife, Cheryl, and serves as senior pastor of Faith Bible Church. He and his wife have two married sons and four grandchildren.

JEFF KINLEY (ThM, Dallas Theological Seminary) has authored more than thirty-five books and speaks across the United States. His weekly podcasts—*The Vintage Truth Podcast* and *The Prophecy Pros Podcast* with Todd Hampson—are heard in more than one hundred countries. Jeff and his wife live in Little Rock, Arkansas, and have three grown sons. His website is Jeffkinley.com.